Di[illegible] s II
Men[illegible] Child

Mike Hupfer

2023

Discarded Darkness II: Memoir of a Broken Child

He summoned me, “Come here Mikey, I’m going to show you some naked pictures of my mom and dad.” I felt duty bound and responded quickly. He had groomed me well.

Chapter 1: Toxic Foundation

Through the eyes of a quiet seven year old kid, it all started when my father’s orange sports car with black mag wheels broke down near a steel mill less than a mile away from our new southern town. For the last time, father got out of his much loved now broken down little sports car and scrunched into the tank that was the family station wagon. Then, we all made our way to the little town and to the new home and to a new start. The sun was still heavy in the sky and the afternoon baked with humidity as we arrived at our new house.

The old house doesn’t have a garage and we parked the station wagon in the cedar planked parking area that has rough hewn gravel as its foundation. The parking area is ideally suited for a couple of small cars and the station wagon is a battle tank. The large two story house is an old Tudor style and it’s surrounded by red clay bricks and broken cobblestone. The rolling meadows of the lawn looked uneven with some clever mole trail networks interspersed throughout the vast yard. Walnut trees and thick prickly bushes dominate the landscape. On the west side of the house, there is a small slab of a mismatched basketball court that has a mangled pole with a crooked rim. About two hundred yards past the basketball court is a crude clumpy garden whose only real success was bringing to life several tiny marijuana plants one homecoming season. The garden is near a section of dilapidated weathered white fencing that separates heavy field brush from the creek that runs parallel to the back of the house.

The same creek becomes a raging river when storms pass through. Towards the back of the house, there is a large concrete sundeck that has a gas grill attached to it. The sundeck is rarely used for anything family related. The sundeck's principal function is for the mass overflow of drunken high schoolers partying at my brother's parties. Rounding out the east side of the house is an unkempt small storage shed located underneath the sundeck's northern slope. The remainder of the lawn is smattered with rough patches and undulating terrain and small bushy prickly shrubbery that circles back around to the front of the house.

At the front of the house, pay close attention to the wide concrete steps leading past the vaulted porch to the sturdy front door. The sturdy front door even has an old fashioned knocker attached to it. After entering the front door, we are greeted by a steep staircase to the left. As we climbed up the staircase, we noticed some pictures were already hung as the movers had finished much of the detailed work along with completing all the heavy lifting. On the top of the stairs, we are greeted by a mostly functional half bathroom. The bathroom always smelled a little bit and was smelly regardless of use. The second floor has three large bedrooms with my parent's room closest to the bathroom. In the time to come, the bedroom is vacant with the cracks of a troubled marriage deepening to a wide chasm of empty darkness. My sister occupies the middle room and my brother and I share the other room. Soon thereafter, my brother moved to the basement and commandeered it like a conquering soldier taking the trophies of war.

As we head back down the stairs to the main floor, we make our way to the living room. Back in the day, the living room was designed as an inviting parlor and a cozy sitting room. Little thought was given to modern annoyances like televisions and entertainment centers. In its current state, the once classy room looks downtrodden and hopelessly barren with few amnesties to help brighten its melancholy.

There is a majestic old sooty fireplace pleading for someone to come spark it to life. In an adjacent room, there is a room designed for use as the family dining room. In the dining room, the eloquent maple table is disrespectfully relegated to warehouse duty and to store large piles of posts and parcels and bills and other random junk. Right across the hall from the dining room is a small den. The den is supposed to be a place to cozy up as a family and watch movies and hang out. Ultimately, the small den becomes my father's sleeping tomb. Step out of the den and into the hallway and then proceed to a dark alcove at the end of the narrow hallway. At the end of the hallway is an eerie green bathroom. During my brother's parties, the green bathroom is used by the high school girls to powder their noses and for other things. Being socially minded, the high school boys use nature for relief. After exiting the bathroom, compose yourself as you enter the kitchen. The kitchen is tight and compact with a little nook and a round table crammed into a corner. During the parties, the kitchen table is used by mother as she is the honored guest. Mother is often surrounded by star struck high school kids and other attendees including an older friend of my sister who I will call Ginocchio. Ginocchio and my mother like to share stories and schnapps and talk about bands from back in the day and that was real music by golly.

Chapter 2: Mangled Tale

Near the kitchen table is the door that leads down to the basement. Go ahead and open the door and then carefully walk past the scary looking fuse box to start the descent down the decrepit creaky narrow stairs until you reach the bottom. At the bottom of the stairs is a dimly lit room that our cat uses as his litter box closet. Unfortunately, the feline's tail was mangled in an accident leaving him with about half of it and we never sought medical attention to fix it.

Pepper's tail healed as a sickening stump resembling a disjointed appendage and I was hesitant on petting him for fear of raising the stump. The family ship was sinking and it was everyone for himself including Pepper.

About one hundred yards from the litter box room is a much larger room which houses a giant hissing boiler that produces blinding hot water for the old fashioned radiators scattered throughout the house. Mother was absolutely terrified of the boiler room, so I used the room to escape from her when necessary.

The rest of the basement was open and ran the entire length of the foundation. My brother and I initially shared a bedroom on the second floor. Not long after that, he moved to the large partitioned part of the basement that landed east to west. It was a huge room that ran the entire length of the basement and was a considerable upgrade from bunking with me.

So, just like that, my brother, this high school kid, had his own basement apartment with its own private entrance. My brother furnished his basement apartment with all the traditional things like couches and tables and chairs and lamps and rugs and a bachelors bed and some other things. Naturally, he decorated the way a high school kid would with music posters and girly pinups and vintage albums on the wall. Now, just add beer.

Chapter 3: Baked Alaska

My parents married young after mother got pregnant. Of course, many youngsters get married young for similar reasons. It was a different time with societal pressure and expectations for that type of thing. Before getting married, my parents didn't have much time individually to be irresponsible and reckless and to learn and grow from that experience. They both brought that emotional inexperience and a tenuous bond as a couple into their marriage and then into our family allowing instability to fester from the start.

That instability created a toxic ointment that was spread onto us kids. The pinnacle of this toxic emotional inexperience was on display with the wild high school keg parties that my older brother was allowed to host. My brother was the party master and mother was his assistant as she would purchase the sixteen gallon kegs for the parties.

In this small town, the parties that my brother hosted were huge in scale and legendary and everybody knew about them. Dozens of intoxicated high school girls and boys were scattered throughout the basement with the overflowing masses of teenagers spilling out into the backyard and onto the sundeck and down to the basketball court. To commemorate the event, group photos of high school girls and high school boys were taken. With an abundance of alcohol consumed, fights ensued and sexuality explored and some logs were burned too.

Mainly though, these were just small town high school kids getting wasted and being loud and grinding to the beat and smoking some weed and occasionally getting out of their shorts. The cool kids are granted access into my brother's private basement chamber and these kids had the best pot and the hottest girlfriends and the least reservations about sharing.

Mother not only bought the beer for the party, but also attended it. Mother hung around just up the stairs from the party and sat in the nook close to the refrigerator. Mother preferred southern schnapps and her southern schnapps was always served on the rocks thank you very much. Normally, mother was surrounded by star struck high schoolers who thought she was cooler than Baked Alaska.

To appear in command, mother would occasionally try to hunt me down to make sure I wasn't getting too drunk. It was a comical scene watching mother careening through hordes of drunken underage high-schoolers trying to find me. As ridiculous as it sounds, I played her like an air guitar. If I needed a quick escape, I hid in the boiler room as mother was terrified of it. From fourth grade onward, I drank as much as I wanted with impunity.

Chapter 4: Swim with the Snakes

The little southern town we moved to has a lot of history. In one form or another, the little town had been around since the early 1800's. Coal mining was the foundation of its existence then and still played an important function now. Like many small towns, there was little in the way of industry or adventure, so hard drinking was woven into the fabric of daily life. At first glance, a person passing through wouldn't describe this small town as particularly prosperous looking. The small town did possess some unique charm though. The narrow main street had a couple of antique dime stores, an old fashioned bank, a small cafe, a pool hall, a barber shop, a small bakery, several churches, and numerous drinking establishments. Additionally, the small town had a cascading system of intertwined creeks and gorges. Finally, there was a grand Victorian styled high school that served surrounding communities. Whatever charm that existed in the small town was unintentionally siphoned by a churning of negative energy created by maladjustments and hardships and misfortunes.

For many generations, coal mining helped to sustain the populace of this town and many other surrounding towns. Even though coal mining had decreased, it was still a big economic player. Of course, coal mining is a hard life for all who touch it and heavy drinking is an accepted coping mechanism for coal mining and most other small town hardships for that matter. One source of pride for the town, however, is its annual homecoming. Traditionally, homecoming was a welcome back to the miners who have been away from home facing the challenges and dangers of coal mining. For homecoming, the main street is shut down and filled with carnival rides and amusements and colorful festivities and loud music and beer tents in full gallop. For a few days, the town coalesces for a warped sense of togetherness cemented by heavy drinking and a chaotic flow of energy and the feeling that everything is going to be okay for a little while and a few days later, it's over.

When we moved to the little southern town, I was an innocent seven year old kid. I had a couple months to get settled in before starting the third grade. The first people I had any interaction with were the neighbors who lived across the street. I will call the neighbors the Strano Family. The Strano Family's patriarch was a soft spoken coal miner who provided well for his family. They lived in a nice home and from outward appearance anyway, everything seemed in order. The Strano Family was religious and practiced it with genuine zealotry. The Strano Family's matriarch was on the lookout for people who needed saving and my family made her list of "families needing saving" as evidenced by her scribbling on a pad of paper. Most of my family managed to avoid the Strano Family entirely. Mother was not as slick and got both herself and myself sucked into that vortex of religious zealotry. The Strano Family's matriarch was a domineering woman and mother never really stood much of a chance pushing back. A couple of times mother and I were browbeat into going to Strano's church. We spent the whole afternoon participating in all types of religious education and witnessing spiritual idolatry.

Our own family was minimally practicing Catholics and the concept of church service lasting past an hour was more terrifying than the devil himself. After a short time, the Strano family matriarch arranged sleepovers for me and the Strano's only daughter who was older than me. The Strano family had a son about my age, so I thought the whole sleepover arrangement with the daughter was off from the start.

I wanted mother to intervene and cancel the sleepovers but she couldn't stand up to the domineering Strano matriarch. When I would stay over, I slept in their daughter's bedroom. The daughter invited me to sleep in bed with her and she wasn't as pushy as her mother but she still had some similar traits. I was terrified of the situation that I found myself locked into. Looking back, I believe that arrangement was mapped out by the Strano matriarch for the purpose of manipulating a religious proselytizing with the daughter being used as bait, like bundling youngsters to let sexually immature kids experiment and letting curiosity take its course.

After my brother's keg parties first started roaring to life, the alcohol devil came to my rescue. The Strano Family's matriarch cut off all connections with us as we were now beyond saving. God bless the devil.

Chapter 5: Mind Cage

As I would learn, the real danger lived down the street. When I was playing in our backyard one sunny afternoon, I met him. He was walking by and came over and introduced himself. I discovered that he was one of the members of a family that I will call the Pericoloso Family. He told me where they lived and that I should stop down there and I did.

The family was typical for the area. They were heavy drinkers and good natured and friendly and not particularly stable emotionally and financially. The father of the family was a jovial fellow who liked spicy chili and driving trucks and watching professional wrestling and watching other things.

When he was drunk, the father would place furniture on top of his children and me as he was replicating the intricate complexities of professional wrestling. I don't think he meant any harm by it. He was just really drunk and the idea presented itself into a clouded mind cage.

The mother of the family was a free spirit who loved to dance and smoke grass and take dirty pictures of herself and her husband. She was usually in a festive mood and was quick to smile and laugh and was able to craftily distract her husband from his intoxicated malfeasance.

Through the years leading up to high school, I was friends with another Pericoloso sibling. We hung out together and liberated alcohol from our families and paid nasty dogs to purchase booze for us and some other things. My intense friend was conniving and resourceful and methodical and charming. I'm confident I know why some of the schemes were devised in the first place.

Particularly when he was drunk, my intense friend had almost no filter. My intense friend carried himself in a rather stern fashion and wasn't much for catering to people's feelings except when catering was useful. Catering was useful with a friend of ours whose father owned a restaurant. That friend could get us bottles of booze as easily as walking in the restaurant and walking out with some bottles of booze.

My intense friend and I got into some trouble together and nothing serious. It was mainly the mania of getting drunk and fighting each other and fighting other people and hazing police cars and rolling abandoned cars into the drinking pond.

As a solo actor, my intense friend allegedly set a fire in our shed below the sundeck and it was a big thing as the shed fire started to burn the back entrance to our house and it was a close call. Someone said they saw him running from the shed and it was never proven and it wouldn't have mattered to me anyway.

With my intense friend, I saw some of the dark pieces of his personality and he had a tenuous grip on reality sometimes. In large part, that is what drew me to him as his mental cannon was loaded and ready to fire and in your face and what are you going to do about it type of attitude and he wasn't playing.

My mental cannon was buried deep in the recesses of my brain and it was mostly unloaded and usually under control. My intense friend and I shared many exploratory experiences including some using drugs like acid and some random pills and some other things. It's impossible to know what pills we used specifically.

We got them and we used them and we had a knack for getting things one way or another. As youngsters, my intense friend and I would sell vitamins to neighbor kids and present them as some exotic drug. The wicked pills we gulped down were not vitamins with some of them generating terrifying side effects.

Up until I started high school, my intense friend remained tenuous friends. We occasionally ran into each other and shared some memories and some drinks and some other things.

When I moved, we never communicated again.

Chapter 6: Ragweed Porn

When we moved to the small southern town, I started my academics as a third grader. For one year, my sister and I both attended the same catholic school that had a beautiful large church. Our family was not religious in the least and it didn't matter. For my sister and me, that year was the last year of what would resemble normalcy and even that year wasn't without disaster. The following year, we both were transplanted to the public school system with my sister entering the trenches of high school. After attending catholic school together, my sister and I rarely interacted other than as meandering participants at random parties including my brother's own basement parties. Growing up, my sister and I never meshed and the lack of connection as siblings and the toxic family system made us almost total strangers then and we're almost total strangers now even after all these years.

Around the time I was finishing the third grade, I started to hang around the Pericoloso family more and sometimes slept there overnight. The Pericoloso family had alcohol fueled parties often showing porn movies. These porn movies were shown in plain sight for everybody to witness including us house kids and the other kids brought over by the invited friends. When I first saw these movies, I was mostly confused and didn't know what was going on. I looked to the adults for direction and guidance but the adults were too busy hollering and drinking and making out and watching the porn actors do what they do in these types of movies.

Additionally, there was an old projector in the basement with a box full of dirty movies and this particular collection of porn was especially nasty and the collection was not quite hidden but put away to the side by the coffee can filled with homemade grass. Sometimes the grass was good, and other times, it was just ragweed.

Over the course of the next few months, my intense friend and I hung out a lot. Naturally, I got to hang around his other siblings too, particularly one. This sibling was always interested in hanging around us and seemed to take a special interest in me. This sibling usually had some really good pot too.

When the parents were gone, this sibling would let us do anything we wanted, not that we didn't already. We drank some mad dog and drank some beer and drank some booze and smoked some weed and listened to some music and cooked some bacon to satiate our pot fueled munchies.

This sibling considered himself a musician, so he would play some music and put on a show and take off his shirt and shriek loudly and dance around and jump up and down like any respectable rockstar would do. This sibling was always fun and goofy and carefree and gave me a lot of attention and made it fun to be around him.

Looking back now, I know what he was doing. I was being groomed to be used when the time was right.

Chapter 7: Family Tomb

In some ways, my parents were kids themselves when they got married. Before we moved to this small town, cracks in my parent's marriage had already started to surface.

After my brother was born, mother received a lot of help with child rearing. From early on, our grandparents and aunts and uncles and family friends all played a prominent role in the rearing. While well intended, all that help didn't push mother to better master the role of mother or my father too for that matter. On top of that, neither one of my parents took the time to better learn the nuisances and challenges of being a parent. When my parents started having children of their own, I believe they wanted to abandon ship and on a subconscious level resented the end of their own carefree adolescence. I don't believe either of my parents advanced emotionally beyond the period of time leading up to their marriage and any coping strategies they had developed didn't advance as they got older.

Mother was brought up in a household where my grandfather was the breadwinner and my grandmother took care of the kids. It was a comfortable childhood for mother and her siblings and she was a little spoiled being the only daughter. Mother likely envisioned that she would follow in the same type of arrangement as my grandmother. My father's childhood was decidedly more complicated. His family didn't provide much of a blueprint so he followed the societal template of the day and the blueprint was that a man worked and tried to provide for his family and the wife took care of the kids.

Chances are that neither one of my parents ever felt entirely comfortable in their roles as parents. They didn't commit to much more and ended up defaulting to what they had already learned. At that stage in their lives, their emotional intelligence and coping mechanisms were basic.

The rudimentary emotional intelligence was on display at the keg parties propagated under my parent's tutelage. My parents allowed my older brother, a high school kid, to throw huge drinking parties for scores of high school students and our house became party central. My mother bought the kegs of beer and was an active participant. Both of my parents, however, were culpable as they allowed this to fester in the first place.

Not long after we moved to the small southern town, both of my parents started flea bagging. Neither of my parents had any problem finding flea ridden hounds either. Whatever flea bagging my dad did was mostly hidden from us and we never knew the entire story. Mother's flea bagging was not a secret to most people and definitely not to us kids.

At a dive bar in a town nearby, mother introduced us kids to a person who I will call Vincent. Vincent bought us some booze laden ice cream grasshoppers and we all got buzzed up along with Vincent and mother. I got to skip grade school the next day, so my first impression of Vincent was a positive one.

Mother met Vincent at a restaurant she worked at one town over and this town was doing well as the west tip of the city was right off the interstate. At that time, Vincent appeared to be a successful salesman and traveled to cities throughout the state and Vincent happened to be staying at the same hotel where my mother worked as a waitress.

Mother often told the story of how Vincent captured her heart. It seems ridiculous now and love is crazy sometimes. As the story goes, Vincent told mother that he liked the way she walked as she was serving him lunch. Apparently, it was love at first sight and love is blind. At that time, Vincent seemed to have all the trappings of success, including nice clothes and coiffed hair and a nice truck and the air of confidence of a man who is doing well. When state regulations were codified, however, all that changed for Vincent.

The modifications nearly eliminated the requirement for the type of heavy duty equipment that Vincent sold. Vincent was fired and didn't have a back-up plan and became a vagabond sleeping in basements and in his truck and in hotels and wherever he could find refuge. With mother tagging me along, I remember visiting Vincent when he stayed in the basement of a bar friend of his.

Vincent was proud of his ruggedness and took showers outside with cold water from an outside hose, wearing just his shorts and not much else. Vincent didn't care that the neighbors saw him undressing and lathering up and keeping his shorts on and not much else.

Vincent could be charming and was an affable guy who was outgoing and good looking and fit. Still, something was off with Vincent.

Even before Vincent entered the picture, I knew something was wrong with my parents. My parents had some boisterous outbursts but not many. It was the house that betrayed the marital carnage. The house had an unnerving feel of a chilled morgue with quiet terror and misery with suffering creatures living somewhere inside. There were obvious signs of marriage woes like when my dad moved from their upstairs bedroom to a small den downstairs.

When my father closed the door to the den, he effectively shut himself off from everybody. My father did almost everything in the den and didn't really come out much except to go to work. My father's den tomb had a television and a couple of chairs and a table and a really small mattress.

My father would occasionally ask me to sit with him and watch television. The den was smoky and smelly and sad and I couldn't wait to get out of there. The family descended into the dark recesses of inhospitable catacombs and was in crisis and everybody lived independent of one another. The isolation grew toxic mold that mutated through the years.

All the family's dirty debris drained into the septic of toxic contamination and my sister became the family scapegoat. My sister forcibly took all the family shame and destruction onto her shoulders and she acted out a lot. My sister and mother fought violently as competitors and enemies. The vicious fighting was nothing resembling a mother and daughter relationship. It was horrifying to witness and visible for all to see.

Essentially, my sister was taking an awful beating for the family and it was all for nothing. By that time, the family as a unit was nearly dead and everybody was abandoning the plague infested family ship.

Mother had stopped coming home and my father isolated himself into the den tomb even more.

Mother's fleabag boyfriend Vincent was a volatile source of contention for a marriage that was already in free fall. At different stages, both of my parents were flea baggers. By making little effort to hide Vincent, I suspect mother was trying to stick it to my father. Mother would often tag me along when she visited Vincent.

Now, mother was meeting Vincent in our little hometown where everybody knew somebody. One time, my father came into the same restaurant where Vincent, mother and I were having lunch. My father saw us and then walked right out. I felt really bad for my father and felt that I somehow had betrayed him. I hated mother for using me to stick it to my father and this wouldn't be the last time either.

To avenge mother's conspicuous flea bagging with Vincent, my father romanced a younger woman and they briefly courted. After the divorce was final, my father married the younger woman. Not long before my dad got remarried, the family house was put up for sale.

After the house was put up for sale, the family disbanded and we all splintered apart from there.

Chapter 8: Rotten Waters

After the family splintered, I was gifted to mother and she used me for leverage in the divorce proceedings with child support bringing income to the coffers. Mother thought it would be a good idea for us to live with Vincent.

At that point, Vincent was a skilled vagabond and couldn't really take care of himself, let alone mother and me. Mother knew that and it didn't seem to matter to her and maybe love is blind. At the time, Vincent was managing a bankrupt resort that I'll call the Lake of the Seven Fingers.

At one point in its history, the resort was a beautiful oasis and a beacon of serenity and a popular vacation destination and was located within driving distance of a large metropolitan city. Now, it's an empty shell of its glory days. The crippled resort still has some swagger and offers some fishing and some camping and some drinking and some opportunities for whole scale drinking. According to Vincent, he used all his salesman wiles and convinced the absentee resort owners to put their trust in him. He assured them that he was up to the challenge of managing the property and it should be an easy task as most of the resort was now an abandoned shell. Vincent thought of himself as a smooth talker and liked to think that his smooth talking is the reason the resort owners hired him in the first place.

I think they hired Vincent because he was cheap labor and they couldn't find anyone else to do it. The resort was desolate and bleak in areas and had the feel of a ghost town. The absentee owners lived out of state and were trying to sell the resort as quickly as possible. Before mother and I moved there, Vicent was managing the resort for about six months.

During that period, mother would drag me with her in the dead of the night to visit Vincent and they would spend some time together. Vincent wasn't mean to me most of the time. I wasn't his kid and I was just in the way of his shady romance with mother.

After the family house was put up for sale, we moved to the resort to live with Vincent permanently.

When I arrived at the resort, the scene was apocalyptic. The once fine dining restaurant was burned significantly and still appeared to smolder a little bit in spots. Mother worked at the restaurant and she got to see Vincent plus the tips were good and I got dragged there too sometimes. It was an open secret that the restaurant was not making money. The restaurant owner was a big time drinker and told anyone who would listen that he was losing money. When he was drunk, he would spin a tale of how much he wanted to see a campfire and that he missed roasting his nuts. Nobody knew what he meant and just laughed him off as a drunken fool talking gibberish.

Not too long before mother and I moved to the resort, the once beautiful restaurant burned down one morning. My friends and I snooped around the charred remains of the restaurant looking for booze and it was a little dangerous to be doing that as debris and remnants would sometimes collapse a little and the burned heap of whatever remained was probably toxic too. In the back of what remained of the restaurant was a now disfigured little suspension bridge.

The bridge carried you over the mouth of the restaurant's lake to a once pristine luxury mini golf course. The mini golf course was damaged by flying chars of burning debris and was marred a lot but not entirely. My friends and I wouldn't spend a whole lot of time in the burned restaurant or at the mini golf course. The area was a mess and it smelled horrible and the bridge to cross over to the mini golf course was in bad shape and scary to cross.

Let's take a walk down this meandering road together. At the resort, it's the only road that takes you anywhere. The road eventually leads you to where we lived at the lodge. After passing by the burned shell of the restaurant, the next facility is a large cedar planked watershed. The watershed is very large as it houses a huge holding tank and two large industrial pumps with one pump taking lake water to the holding tank and the other to pump transporting the water to just the lodge now as the pool complex has been out of action for a while.

Less than a quarter of a mile from the watershed is what remains of the pool complex's parking lot. By now, any demarcations of individual parking stalls have long since faded away. The abandoned pool complex itself was not secured or protected from intruders.

My friends and I entered the front door of the pool complex by pushing it open. The pool complex was at best creepy and the rest of the time downright terrifying with odd creatures that either died inside or something else.

The pool complex had a disturbing vibe. It felt like people were just there and had just left and the old signage from the pool complex's glory days were still hanging adding to the horror. I think if we were all blind, we would see the surrounding presence of the spirits.

All of my friends vowed to not go inside alone and we didn't except for that one time when I did and looked around and explored and went through the shower and locker rooms and saw swim trunks and shirts and shorts and pool toys and dead animals. All of this stuff was partially buried by layered mounds of debris and concrete rubble and sediment and sand and I freaked out and stood frozen for a moment and then walked out still mentally paralyzed by fear. I later postulated that I was a bit drunk and the pot was potent and I didn't do acid until later in life. My friends and I would venture out by the large pool and it was dirty and broken and creepy and we would run out the back near the diving board to the safety of the lodge.

That brings us to the lodge. The lodge was a solid structure with thick cedar planks filling every crevice. It was surrounded by acres of mainly unspoiled nature. The lodge had fourteen large rooms with many modern conveniences.

I had my own room and it had a huge bed, a large bathroom with a shower, a nice sitting area with some tables and chairs, a few old style lamps, a microwave, a little refrigerator, a moderate sized television, a booming stereo system and a huge heavy couch that folded out into another large bed.

My room was at the extreme end of the lodge and it was far away from mother and Vincent. I did my own thing and grew distant from mother and Vincent.

Other than occasional meals with them, I was on my own almost all the time.

At the resort, the lodge was the only thing still operational and it was rare for weary travelers to actually stay there. The lodge was not advertised and it was not easy to find. Besides the three of us, the majority of the people who stayed there were Vincent's friends and family who exploited the resort for the weekend normally.

Vincent rarely charged friends or family who stayed at the lodge or who used the grounds to camp and the people who did insist on paying would have to pay cash as there was not a system in place to take credit card payments and Vincent would pocket the cash. Vincent justified the theft as a means to help offset his meager salary as the property manager.

Vincent took advantage of the fact that the resort owners lived out of state. I think Vincent wanted to show off and play the role of a wealthy landowner.

On weekends, Vincent invited hoards of disturbed people to the resort to party and get drunk and exploit the lake and campgrounds and other people and it was a nasty circus with whole dead pigs spinning and cooking in a special grill and slimy people getting drunk and taking off their clothes and falling into fire pits and passing out.

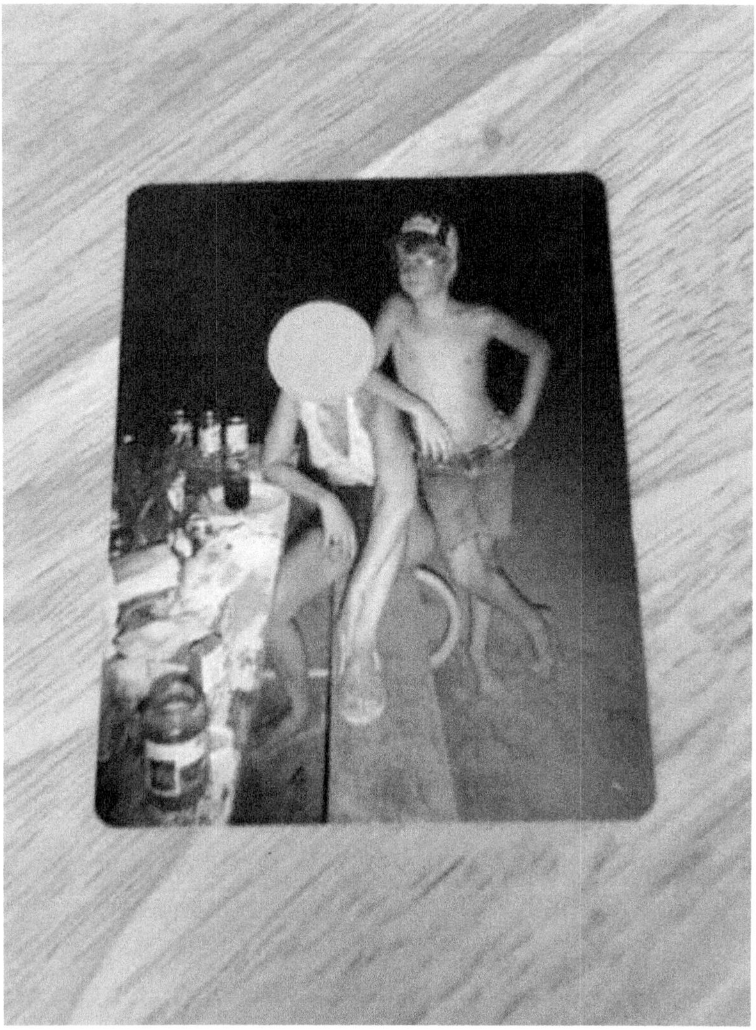

These ugly moments changed me piece by piece. After seeing mother in that disgusting circus environment so often, I grew to disrespect her and Vincent. The great irony is as the resort's property manager, Vincent didn't do a whole lot of actual property manager work and some of the work that

Vincent did try to complete was nearly a disaster. All the time claiming he was well versed in the principals of controlled burning, Vincent nearly caused a forest fire. Vincent started many little fires that soon became a lot bigger and Vincent got us in serious trouble quickly. Fortune smiled on us that day and we were saved by a change in wind direction.

After we moved to the resort, I had some time to get settled. It would be a couple months before starting the seventh grade. I would be starting at a new school and a new town and a new everything. On the weekends, my other town friends would come to the resort. I became a popular guy with the word spreading that I had my own place at some cool abandoned resort.

My other town friends and I had already established a reliable network of fee based booze gatherers and we had developed the network over the years. Collectively, our booze of choice was Mad Dog 20/20 and that stuff is nasty and potent. We would buy as much as we could hide and bring some pot too. We hardly ever ran out of booze and if we did Vincent had plenty of beer. Vincent would complain that people would steal beer from the outside refrigerator and that was wrong because he likes his beer ice cold and the inside refrigerator just doesn't get beer cold enough.

When I started the seventh grade, I wasn't trying to make any new friends. The kids there really didn't give me much of a hard time and some did and not many and I kept to myself and I was a disturbed quiet kid and all the violations and chaos and abandonment and family animosity had rattled my marbles. I made it through the seventh grade mostly unscathed and didn't have any issues academically or with many kids bullying me and I had joined the school basketball team and never played much and the fortunes at the resort were about to deteriorate.

At one point, extended family from out of state stayed at the resort for the weekend. The following day after they left, the power was shut off. Vincent hadn't paid the power bill for a few months and he strung the power company along for awhile and they finally realized he was full of crap and cut ties with him and cut the power.

Not having electricity was problematic for many reasons, not the least of which we now had no running water as the electric pumps that supplied the water could not pump. Being an experienced vagabond, Vincent explained that the no electricity situation was not a problem and we would bathe in the lakes for the cleaning and haul water to fill the toilets for the bathrooming and use lanterns for the lighting and use the grill for the eating and use the blankets and kerosene heaters for the warming. So simple, he said, even a child could do it.

After several months of not having electricity, the resort was reported for environmental infractions and the authorities tracked down the absentee owners who eventually contacted Vincent. About three weeks later, the absentee resort owners returned to our state and then to the resort. The absentee owners fired Vincent in person and we were evicted from the lodge.

Chapter 9: Predator

After being evicted from the resort, neither mother, nor Vincent, had any real plan to get us a place to live and they didn't have the money or the creative resources or the constructive dialogue to brainstorm possible solutions anyway. When nobody else would take them in, they were fortunate that a kindly impoverished family, who I will call the Carnone Family, agreed to let them live with them. I knew the Carnone Family well because mother and Vincent tricked me into staying with them overnight a few times when they would go out of town or when they wanted to be away from me. The patriarch of the Carnone Family was a friendly fellow who was a reluctant coal miner by trade. Instead of coal mining, he preferred drinking beer much of the day and ended up losing part of his foot as he continued drinking heavily against medical advice with his diabetes and got on a lacking part of the foot disability and effectively retired from coal mining.

The Carnone Family had a son who I will call George. George was the eldest of the boys and was severely physically and mentally impaired. I felt bad for George and I didn't like him and he scared me and it wasn't his fault. George's life was made challenging with complications during his delivery. The Carnone Family never sued the hospital and chalked it up to God's will. George could not walk or talk and his communication was limited to screaming and hitting himself in the head and giggling and shrieking and a combination of screaming, shrieking and hitting his head. George was strapped in a specialized padded wheeled chair nearly all the time and he was sinewy and loud and smelled like pee and I didn't like George and he scared me and it wasn't his fault.

When mother and Vincent wanted to get away from the responsibilities of running an abandoned resort, they would escape and leave the city. The Carnone Family was a convenient choice to watch me even though I lived independent of those fools and had from the very beginning. As the car started to climb up the Carnone Family's steep rocky driveway, I sometimes didn't realize what they were up to until it was too late. I would always run away, just not that far and mother would lure me back. I wish I was more disobedient as I already disrespected mother and Vincent and this just added to the fire. When I stayed overnight at the Carnone's house, I slept in the same pee stenched bedroom as George and the other brothers on the bottom bunk right across from George who had a chambered bed and George would scream and shriek and giggle and sleep then shriek and wake up and I hated mother and Vincent and George and it wasn't George's fault. In the end, the Carnone Family were generous people and allowed mother and Vincent to live with them for over a year.

Mother and Vincent were lucky as nobody else wanted to take them in and it's better to leave trash at the curb.

After being evicted from the resort, I was returned to live at the family home in the other town. I soon would be starting the eighth grade and reconnecting with some classmates. By now, I was eerily quiet and smiled when I had to and became more disturbed on the inside. The family as a unit was already dead and the family house was listed for sale and would be sold to a grade school teacher. My dad had already moved onto the next family and the next house and the next town and wasn't around much and neither was anybody else for that matter. The house was unsettlingly quiet yet strangely chaotic like it knew the time had come. It was in this transition period that I started to feel much of the sadness and pain with the death of the family. The sadness quickly grew into intense anger and I turned that anger inward steering myself down a horribly dark twisted path. I kept all that buried and I wanted people to like me so I presented a happy version of myself to the outside world.

During this period, I was drinking to excess and remember going to the bus stop still intoxicated from the night before and fortunately eighth graders sober up fast. I was drinking to get drunk to make those feelings go away and they never did for very long. I went to a lot of parties and it was during one particularly wild party that I met up with some old friends and some other people and we all decided to try acid. My intense friend was there too and he appeared even more unbalanced than before. With my intense friend by my side, I felt safe and confident to try new drugs or pills or booze or whatever. Before this adventure, we both explored many things together, so this little trip was child's play.

As luck would have it, acid was now being sold by a dealer who primarily sold weed and she asked if we would like to buy some acid and we bought ten little cardboard squares for a group trip. We all spent hours tripping and drinking beer and didn't seem to get drunk and most of us had a good trip as far as tripping goes.

Before that drug fueled party, I started to have nightmares about what had happened at the hands of the predator. When the nightmares started, I drank myself blind in an attempt to bury the memory. No matter what I did, I couldn't forget what happened when I was a little kid. The chain of events played over in my head and I couldn't shut off the recording.

No matter how much I drank, I couldn't forget that fateful day.

That fateful day started one Saturday morning when I walked over to the predator's family home. When I got there, I knocked on the door and let myself in as was the custom. The predator saw me coming and greeted me with a warm hello and a big grin. After a while, we all smoked some weed, and not the coffee can stuff, but the predator's pot and it was potent skunk weed. We all rocked to some music and ran around a little and then smoked some more weed. The predator's parents were not home and we did anything we wanted with the predator leading the way. He showed us pictures of himself and his friends and other people who seemed to be unaware that their picture was being taken. Some of the pictures showed people in stages of undress with some of the people naked and some as a group and he presented the pictures as a type of art exhibition in a large metropolitan city. The predator told us that he is an artist and a musician and a photographer and he always seemed to know what to say. During the months I spent over at their house, the predator paid me a lot of attention and some of it seemed artificial and I didn't care and I liked to be around him and his siblings and having access to the booze and the pot too. After smoking even more skunk weed, we all played a game of hide and seek and the whole house came into play and there were no boundaries and the predator fetched some pictures of his parents that were scattered about on the top of their dresser.

He summoned me, “Come here Mikey, I'm going to show you some naked pictures of my mom and dad.” I felt duty bound and responded quickly. He had groomed me well.

For a little kid, the pictures of his parents were unsettling and gross. Both his mom and dad were entirely naked and they both were smiling wildly with their private parts in full view and in hideous detail and as he showed me the pictures, the predator was smiling too.

He then commanded, “Now, you have to do something for me.”

By that time, I was emotionally numb and was monstrously stoned and the pot induced paranoia just shelled me in further.

He then commanded, “Now, I'm taking you all down to the basement and we're going to watch a movie.”

When we got down to the basement, a horrible porn movie was already playing. The predator then turned on the ancillary purple lights and the large pot fan and then turned off the other lights. He then turned up the volume of the porn movie and seated the other siblings right in front of the television and told them to look straight ahead and then took me to the back part of the basement and pulled down my shorts and underwear and I went limp and died a little and never told anyone.

Chapter 10: Trailer Trash

After we were evicted from the resort, I rarely saw mother or Vincent when they were staying with the Carnone family.

After about a year, Vincent found us a place to live and it was a horrible avocado rental home. Including this green one, the husband and wife team owned some other rental properties. Vincent was convinced that he sold them on the idea that he was a skilled carpenter and that his expertise could be used to maintain and fix their other rental properties or their home and that he could work his carpentry magic and that could help offset the rent if it ever came down to it.

The husband and wife owners were likely dubious of Vincent's claim given the fact that Vincent didn't have a work truck or even his own car. I don't think the owners really cared all that much as carpenters were in short supply and Vincent could be a source of discounted carpentry services. For the owners, there was little risk as that rental house we lived in was bought on the cheap and they minimally made it fit for human habitability. I thought of it like it was a human dog house with troubled people viewed as trash living inside.

What the rental property owners discovered was that Vincent was learning carpentry as he moved from one job to the next and sometimes his carpentry work was okay and other times, Vincent got in over his head and couldn't complete the project on his own leaving the project unfinished.

After that discovery, the property owners used Vincent's carpentry service a lot less and subsequently the rent was late a lot more when Vincent couldn't exchange his carpentry services for rent. I remember the wife owner regularly knocking on our disfigured front door demanding the rent money and she wore the pants in the family. I was told not to answer the door and I did anyway and I didn't care and I didn't respect mother or Vincent.

With the money I earned from my paper route, I was really the only person with a steady income plus the money from the child support that seemed to support other things. One time, I overheard Vincent and mother talking about the child support money and that they were waiting on it because Vincent needed some tools for his carpentry business. Mother and Vincent were both troubled and living like that would do it. Living like that would also warp emotions and perceptions and behaviors. Mother knew I was disturbed and had been for a long time. The truth was that I was being kept around as a commodity for child support as they both needed the steady flow of money and there was little connection other than that.

When we moved into the human dog house, it was close to the start of my freshman year of high school. By that time, I had started drinking a lot of cheap whiskey and the hard stuff got me to some really dark places. Most of my contemporaries didn't share my taste for the hard stuff, so I hung out with people older than me more often than not.

Even as a little kid, older people liked to hang around me as my intellect and quick wit entertained them. I made people feel good about themselves and could drink a lot without acting too foolish and this continued on through all of high school. I had a small group of contemporaries who I hung out with.

The rest of the drinking hours were spent with older people and most of them weren't exactly extracting life's precious mineral deposits. To be fair, some of those people were decent enough and they just got caught up in this small town's quagmire of misery and suffering and just wanted to forget about that for a while with drinks and drugs.

Throughout high school, I didn't skip out of school all that much. When I did, it was usually with a group of hooligans and we would spend the day drinking and hanging out at an abandoned coal mine. Skipping out of school was tedious to me. I preferred being busy at school and getting high at lunch and going to study hall. School was an easy place to be quiet and to hide. At the start of my senior year, however, the attendance balance sheet was shattered as I skipped out about half my senior year.

In the break following my junior year, I was always on the hunt for a party and could easily find one with the small town word of mouth version of instant messaging. At one large party, I met a person who I will call Tom. Tom and I struck up a conversation and became fast acquaintances. By the time I got to this party, I was already drunk as I was drinking whiskey earlier. When I drank a lot of whiskey, I would become combative and aggressive and Tom seemed to like that.

Tom explained that he deals in weed, occasionally some coke, and more recently magic mushrooms. I've heard of magic mushrooms before and thought they were a watered down version of acid and I used acid before and considered myself a bit of an expert.

Tom assured me that the mushrooms he sells have the potency to give you a trip every bit as good as acid and it's even better than acid because you don't have to commit to hours of tripping. Tom's sales pitch sold me and I assured him that I would be in touch when school started. Tom told me where he lived and I knew what car lot he meant and it was the house right next to it.

The first weekend after school started, I walked over to Tom's house. He didn't tell me that he was couch crashing at his sister and brother-in-law's house and had been doing that for awhile. Tom explained that he has this really cool arrangement where he watched their kid when they went to work and in exchange he got a free place to stay and was able to shoot pool and play ping pong in the basement and was able to deal as long as he was discreet.

Tom knew I loved to play pool and ping pong and that I smoked pot and drank a lot and that I wanted to try mushrooms. Tom suggested that I skip school on Monday and come over in the morning and get high and drink some wine and try some mushrooms and that he would smoke and drink a little too but not too much because he would be babysitting.

Tom said he would keep an eye on me if I wanted to try some mushrooms and he would give me some for free to try and that's where it all began.

So, for the next few months, I set my alarm and woke up early in the morning and got ready and walked out the door and instead of turning right to make the walk to school, I turned the other way and walked the distance to Tom's sister's house. With a knock at his sister's door, I usually woke Tom up and he would leap up from the scratchy green couch to let me in and we did our thing and sometimes well into the night.

At our human dog house, I didn't do anything to conceal the fact that I wasn't attending school. I never had homework or carried books and never talked about school or pretended to have learned anything or ever talked about school functions and never had her sign anything and mother never asked me anything either. My extended school absence was betrayed after the high school principal called mother to see if had succumbed to an illness or if something had happened or if I just decided to quit as leaving school was common in this small town.

A blame game commenced between the principal and mother with the principal chastising mother and pointing out the fact that it's still her responsibility since I'm a minor. Mother was not big on that theory, so she absolved herself and blamed me and that was the end of it.

I returned to high school and was lectured and praised and admonished by educators that I had to pass every class in order to graduate and that education is important and that I had better take it seriously. I rolled my eyes and said everything has been serious for a very long time already. A few weeks later, I was reading magazines in the school library that was part of the large study hall and was passing all my classes with time to spare. I finished the school year with little drama and graduated and threw my cap in the air and was moved out of state not too long thereafter.

Chapter 11: Lunatics

Mother tricked me into thinking we were going on a short trip to visit her parents in another state. Little did I know, the train ride was part of a clandestine action to move me and mother was sneaky when she needed to be. Early one morning, mother and I got on a train in a college town nearby and the train slowly pulled out of the station. It was then a long ride to the great Midwest with many stops along the way.

Hours into the train ride, my mind warped into some kinda hazy chasm of time and space and I drifted off to memory central remembering some of the spirited lunatics I got to know and all the wild times we spent together. One beautiful collection of rabble rousers included a group of cousins and brothers and a miscellaneous collection of misfit toys, including myself. I will call this lunatic fringe the Mais posse. Everyone in the Mais posse was crazy individually and collectively it was bedlam as we all competed to be the craziest. Most everyone in the Mais posse had a vehicle and the competition to be the craziest commenced into the arena of dangerous driving, including how fast one can go and how extreme one would push it. The going fast part was considered easy as we all could drive fast and going really fast could blow an engine and nobody wanted that, so lunatic driving became the principal competition metric.

The eldest member of the Mais posse had a small car and used the car like an all terrain vehicle. The eldest member saw himself as the alpha male, so he had to prove his position in the posse and drove the most extreme by far. To prove my mettle, I often rode with him in the front seat. His driving terrified me and I told him that and he already knew and didn't care and drove more erratically.

In his small car, the eldest member of the Mais posse would try to traverse a steep motorcycle climb hill and would usually get part of the way up, sometimes far up, but he almost always had to roll the car backwards, sometimes coming really close to flipping it over. It was terrifying and sometimes I pissed my pants. I blamed it on the booze but he knew better and tried again and again until the engine of his small car started to overheat and he shut it down right away because nobody wants to blow an engine.

The pinnacle of lunacy for the Mais Posse involved a ride that should have killed us. Besides trying to traverse the motorcycle climb hill, the eldest member of the Mais posse loved to drive through cornfields and did it at night to minimize detection. That fateful night the moon was beautifully full and we were running that little car hard through a cornfield somewhere in the middle of nowhere.

The little car was whipping and smooshing and whacking corn at a frightening pace and I glanced at the speedometer and we were pushing about forty and then looked up to see a huge International Harvester sitting in a clearing coming up and I screamed to "**STOP**" and he locked the brakes and we made it with a few feet to spare.

We sat there for a couple minutes in a state of shock and then we limped the battered little car out of the cornfield and onto a country road and we made it back to town mostly unscathed.

In my circle, the most sordid character in this little town was a person who I will call Salsiccia. Salsiccia is a sibling of a great friend of mine. From outside appearances, Salsiccia looked the part of uncivilized oaf and his slovenly appearance just added to the motif.

If you would talk to him, you knew he wasn't dumb and he could be charming in a goofy sort of way. Salsiccia talked without a filter and in an odd philosophical manner that was a juxtaposition of his uncivilized exterior. Like many people, Salsiccia sold pot and selling pot is common trade in this small town. Salsiccia didn't seem to care what people thought of him and I don't believe he liked people and would describe him as a nihilist.

Salsiccia's passion was dirt bikes. You gave Salsiccia a dirt bike and he became the motorcycle whisperer. Many times, the garage was filled with what seemed like hundreds of motorcycle parts and he often tore down entire dirt bikes and put them all back together. He was the master of all dirt bikes including big dirt bikes. Big dirt bikes were way more motorcycle than I could ever handle, so I rode much smaller dirt bikes.

Salsiccia would take me for a ride on his big two stroke dirt bike and it was very powerful and scary fast. He beefed up the motor's insides and it would go over a hundred miles an hour if given the opportunity. It was terrifying to be a passenger as we went through muddy fields and trails and roads and dams and we never wrecked badly because he was a skilled dirt biker if a bit of a lunatic.

Salsiccia was considered an oddball stoner and didn't have much of a network of contemporaries. Salsiccia hung around some of his siblings and me and a couple other people who used him for pot and when they saw him they would tell him to fire up a joint and we would all get high and they would craftily get rid of him. Salsiccia lacked much emotional intelligence and had difficulty reading people and I tried to help him but he wouldn't listen to me. Salsiccia was a quirky character and lived life by his own philosophy. Salsiccia never gave much credence to what other people thought and that is what drew me to him in the first place. I hung out with Salsiccia through grade school then we both lost contact after he moved away and I moved to the abandoned resort.

Shortly after I started my freshman year of high school, Salsiccia and I reconnected.

Wherever he moved to, Salsiccia had courted a girl and got her pregnant and got her married and they both moved to this little town. Salsiccia moved back to this little town because he needed money to lease a home and needed money for pretty much everything else and he was there to ask for money and he wasn't keen on asking.

Salsiccia had used most of their wedding money to buy weed. His master plan was to turn a tidy profit from the sale of this weed. Realistically, there was little chance of that happening as Salsiccia had become an insatiable pot smoker himself.

On a regular basis, I hung out with Salsiccia and his wife. Salsiccia and I would smoke a bunch of dope and drink some booze and just hang out doing nothing. I felt bad for Salsiccia's wife. He talked loosely with her around to make sure she heard what he was saying and why he chose her and got her pregnant and moved her away from her family. Salsiccia explained that he is the man and she is the woman and that she is there to serve him and that's just how it is. I felt sorry for this visibly pregnant young creature because she took Salsiccia literally. I knew better. Salsiccia was a blowhard and talked philosophically and exoterically to make himself feel bigger.

After she was moved away from her family, Salsiccia's wife was stuck with him. The poor girl didn't know anyone in this town and didn't have any friends and rarely left the home without Salsiccia. At one point, she had managed to stand up for herself but Salsiccia could turn a trump card and lay down a debilitating mind play on demand. Salsiccia wasn't physical with his wife but treated her poorly and treated most people the same way really. I don't believe that Salsiccia ever liked people all that much.

I hung out with Salsiccia to party and because I was a mess. I never wanted a connection with Salsiccia and I didn't care about his idiosyncrasies. Naturally, his young wife desired some sort of connection, so that relationship was probably doomed from the start. Salsiccia treated his wife like an object. When we were done partying for the night, Salsiccia would give me a ride home. As we were leaving out the door, he would admonish her to "assume the position" not so subtly implying that he expects sex when he returns.

For this poor girl, the ugly saga continued for months and the couple's lack of money made it even worse. Salsiccia never made much of an effort to find a regular job and instead doubled down on the failing pot business and that endeavor never had a chance with Salsiccia smoking so much of the inventory. Salsiccia's extended family was through giving him any more money as they saw him squander much of their money on dope. Salsiccia defended his right to run whatever business he saw fit and the dope was necessary for inventory. By this time, Salsiccia was desperate and almost out of cash and had little weed left in inventory.

Salsiccia came up with an unthinkable, yet entirely practical solution in his pot baked eyes: he would return his pregnant wife to her family as he couldn't afford her to take care of her anymore.

I sat in the front seat and rode along during that long trip to drop off his wife. Salsiccia bought a radar detector specifically for the journey and intended on returning it after coming back. Salsiccia borrowed his aunt's car and the aunt came along as she didn't completely trust Salsiccia.

The aunt sat in the backseat along with Salsiccia's wife and the wife was left alone to cry and sleep. We drove hours to the arranged meeting point at the halfway mark. The wife's family met us at a wayside and they sobbed after they saw her and rubbed her belly and Salsiccia hugged his wife a little and that was it. After the road trip, I didn't see Salsiccia very much and we stopped hanging around all together shortly thereafter. A couple months later, Salsiccia moved to parts unknown.

Chapter 12: Dumb Card

As the train got closer to the station, I slumbered around in time to see mother fidgeting with what looked like my birth certificate and I asked her what she was doing with my birth certificate and she said it was something else for her parents. Mother could be crafty and was much more intelligent than she ever let on. She played the dumb card and it became a tool that she used to convince people that she was a victim of circumstance to help distance her culpability from her own poor decisions. I brought one big suitcase for the trip and it had most of the clothes I owned. It was a sad looking brown suitcase and I liked it and it had compartments for my vodka and my cigarettes and my books. Mother said we were visiting her parents for a couple weeks to help them out and get some things out of the basement and to assist with cleaning.

It was just starting to get dark as my uncle arrived to pick us up from the train station. Before he arrived, we waited outside the train depot for about thirty minutes. The train station was located in a rough area of this large city and I thought it was a bad idea to wait outside. After loading the suitcases into the cluttered trunk, we finally got into the safety of my uncle's car and I went into the back seat. From the train station to my grandparent's house, it was about a two hour drive. The drive should have been a pleasant affair as both mother and my uncle were usually chatty and keen on making small talk and this ride had a more serious note and my alerts started to sound. As an abandoned child, my internal alert system had become quite sophisticated and I knew that something was wrong. As the drive continued, an eerie quiet settled in and continued all the way through until reaching my grandparents driveway. When we arrived at my grandparents' large ranch house, they were getting ready for bed and came to the living room to say hello and then good night.

My grandmother was an active and healthy senior who continued to participate in community happenings and shopping and swimming and kept busy and even drove a cool little sporty car. My grandmother could best be described as classy, a testament to the wisdom of her generation. My grandfather was a retired banker and very much from that generation of the heavy smoking and the heavy drinking businessmen who had a couple martinis at lunchtime because that's the way business was done back then. Down the road, that lifestyle caught up with my grandfather and he suffered a stroke that partially paralyzed him and all the smoking led to emphysema. My grandfather was an optimist with a can do attitude and managed to get around okay and drove a large car around town.

For the next few days, mother and I did some of the things she said we would be doing, like helping to clean and helping to organize hundreds of pages of miscellaneous papers and comics and random documents located in the basement and that became my project because it required heavy lifting. I liked the basement as it offered me my own space away from everybody. Through my experiences of living with Vincent and mother, I had become cynical and suspicious of people's motivations for doing things. I didn't trust mother and had the feeling that something was about to happen and I was right. A couple nights later during dinner, mother casually mentioned that they had discussed me living there with her parents, and that my grandparents have agreed to let me live there, but only on a trial basis because they were older and weren't sure if a teenager living with them was going to be a good fit. None of it mattered as the decision was already made. The revelation wasn't a total shock as I suspected something was wrong. Nevertheless, I felt unsettling rage on a subconscious level and had vivid disturbing thoughts about impaling mother with her salad fork. I kept the rage tightly contained and composed myself. I respected my grandparents and didn't want to scare them and I was good at being quiet and it usually protected me.

When it came down to it, I didn't have much choice and I had just moved out of state and I didn't have a car and didn't have much money or clothes. Nobody really understood all the shenanigans mother had pulled and it seemed that nobody particularly cared. In front of her parents, I wanted to ask mother how much of the child support money she had put aside these past six years. Of course, I didn't say a word. The truth was that Vincent and mother used the child support money for things besides my welfare as evidenced by how we lived. After the announcement, I avoided mother as much as possible and made myself nearly invisible by hiding in the basement.

Mother was not comfortable coming down to the basement. I discovered a few strategic areas to hide my booze and I was careful to not get too drunk until later in the evening. I made the basement my little fortress and spent a lot of time down there.

About a week later, Mother left to return home back south. My uncle came to pick her up to take her to the train station and I chose to not ride along. I told everybody I was not feeling well and nobody really believed me and it didn't matter. Everybody was aware that mother and I weren't exactly close and some family attributed that mainly to me but nobody knew the entire story or seemed that interested in my side of the story.

Little did I know then, but mother would return to live with my grandparents permanently.

When I was delivered to my grandparents, none of us really knew each other and we were all just a couple steps up from being strangers really. For the first couple months, it was awkward for all of us. I morphed into my grandparent's routine and helped them with errands and shopping and heavy lifting in the basement and hung out with them a little and tactfully secluded myself in the basement the rest of the time. My primary sleeping room was a small den with a television and a couch that folded out into a bed and I normally slept on the couch as that was easier and the folded out bed took up nearly all usable space in the den anyway. The basement had two small beds and the basement became my satellite bedroom. I used the basement as a kind of apartment and continued nipping on the vodka late at night when everybody was sleeping.

If I wanted to get out of the house, I would just go to some bars nearby. Even though I was underage, getting served in some bars was not particularly difficult. Most bars didn't ask me for anything but money and I liked to spend money on drinks and shots and the jukebox and the darts and the pool table and I could hold my liquor and didn't cause problems. I was quick with the wit and used my southern charm to make people feel comfortable and I was a people pleaser. Now, I understand why I was such a people pleaser. As a kid, I was discarded so much that I internalized this as some type of flaw with me and I wanted people to like me. I didn't allow myself to get too attached to people and seldom made a genuine lasting connection.

My uncle was in real estate and asked me to do odd jobs like cleaning properties and cleaning houses and miscellaneous grunt work. I wish he would have pointed me in the direction of banking or finance or real estate and I don't blame him and he had his own life. His dad was a prominent banker and he was guided in that direction and was a banker himself before getting into real estate. I was sharp and a quick learner and courteous and independent. I suspected that my uncle didn't like the fact that I was living with his parents and that we were connected on some level and that we went to church together and ate dinner together and watched football together. My grandma was a big football fan and I watched football with her and we would cheer and holler but in a buttoned down fashion as my grandmother was a class act even watching football.

My grandfather's post retirement hobby was to deliver an entertainment bundle to family and friends. The bundle included comic strips and miscellaneous items of humor that my grandfather thought would make people smile. The list of people on his delivery route was large and he depended on me as his only staff member. After I became a member of staff, we started to become close. My grandfather and I did that together for a long time before he retired from comic's distribution.

For cash flow, I successfully used the odd job network until a distant cousin reached out and helped me secure a full time gig at a fruit juice factory where she worked. My cousin would pick me up at my grandparent's house and we drove to work together. The juice factory produced thousands of those little boxes of juice. The juice batches were mixed and made in huge caldrons under the purview of people dressed like chemists but who could scarcely divide fractions. The majority of the heavy noise was near these caldrons and most of us were stationed in a sector of production that had a modest level of noise by fruit juice factory standards anyway. My primary job was to pack the juice boxes into rectangular cardboard trays and keep an eye on the glue machine that affixes the little straws to the juice boxes. We were on our feet all day but it wasn't physically demanding work unless you were assigned pallet packing duty. Everyone was laid back and a large part of the production crew was stoned at some point during the night. It was common during lunch for many of us to jump in one guy's van for a couple quick joints and maybe some chips to gobble down. In plain sight, one production supervisor would occasionally lay down on a production table and take a bit of a cat nap and some people groused about it but nobody really cared.

We got paid every week and every Friday a bunch of us would meet at a bar down the street from the juice factory and we would cash our checks and spend some of it on booze and being underage was no matter. There was a married girl who worked at the juice factory and she liked me and liked to flirt and liked to get attention and she joined us too. The napping supervisor joined us and we became acquaintances and we drank together and smoked weed outside of work and sometimes on the weekends. My grandmother would let me borrow her sporty car and I would drive to his apartment and we would drink and smoke weed in great profusion. My juice factory days, however, were coming to an end.

My uncle set-up an interview with a business owner who liked the work I did for him in the odd job network. I showed up for the interview and naturally got the job and was now their sweeper. I wasn't complaining and I was able to retire my juice box. Besides, this is where I met my great friend and everyone called me the sweeper.

Chapter 13: The Sweeper

I was the sweeper at a large industrial manufacturer. Most of the production was centered on skilled welding and niche production laborers with the sweeper at the bottom of the totem pole. My job was to sweep from one end of the factory to the other. With having access to the entire factory, I had the chance to get to know many of the factory workers. As I made my way through the factory, I made my rounds and socialized with all sorts of people and would choose what sectors of the factory I wanted to be around more than the others. I chose to hang around areas where the people were the most interesting or had something to offer. The best group for this was the guys who worked inside the tanks and got high while working. They used one guy as the look out and he sat in the manhole opening to sit guard and it was the only way to get in. I would get into the tank and get high as a kite and then go back to my sweeping rounds.

Impaired sweeping.

One night when the shift was coming to a close, I met the person who would become my great friend and I will call him Rotante. I happened to be sweeping in his little area that night and I started chatting it up with my smartass quips and Rotante threw some jabs back and that was the start of the friendship. After work, we went to a bar frequented by second shifters and we shot some pool and played some darts. Rotante was what I would call a lightweight and one of those rare social drinkers I read about in fables. I was a drunkard having mastered drinking early on as a youngster. Rotante and I gelled because we connected on many levels as outsiders and competed intellectually. Rotante and I became close friends and he would come over to my grandparent's house and hang out and we went clubbing and bar hopping and occasionally ran a little wild in his sports car.

Not long after hanging up my broom, I started attending college at a small school. I didn't have any particular reason to start going to college other than I thought it would be a good idea. I was lacking in direction and attending school didn't change that. It wouldn't have mattered anyway as I was a heavy drinker and any positive direction would have been thwarted by my choice of the bottle.

While attending college, I worked in some retail operations with one large big box store, the most interesting as far as the colorful people I met and the things we did. After work, some of these characters would come over to my grandparents and we would have some drinks with me pounding the whiskey bottle like a little drummer boy. Fortunately, my grandparent's bedroom was at the opposite end of the house and I kept people in line most of the time or we just went outside to the patio. It was kismet as one of my fellow big box co workers lived just a few houses down from my grandparents and his father was a heavy drinker so we would drink there and get drunk with no negative ramifications and the coworker usually had some weed too.

I continued on with school and learned some useful nuggets. One of my business teachers took us on field trips to tour different businesses and I thought that was a great idea. In a psychology class, we got to see a human cadaver and it smelled horrible and looked like most of the parts had been taken already. The most fun I had in college was attending a big city symphony and getting all dressed up and feeling a bit classy for a few hours. I never gelled at this school or desired to live the college life and didn't hang around the college kids outside of class unless we ran into each other at a bar.

At the college graduation ceremony, I walked up to the podium when my name was called and accepted my diploma and kept right on walking out to the back door of the hall. I was followed by confused family members who joined me for the graduation. They didn't know I would be walking out like that and neither did I until that moment. I remember that graduation night well because it was one of the few times my father called me.

My father's life story is convoluted and his life was made challenging and that likely has something to do with his communication style. After we moved to that little southern town, he tombed himself in that little den and closed the door and rarely came out.

Every so often, my father would come down to the basement during my brother's high school keg party to get a taste of human interaction and that got everybody's attention and he could be quite gregarious when pickled.

In his own house, my father lived as a solitary man surrounded by others and then the house was sold and he moved away to another house and to another life. I occasionally stayed overnight with my father and his new wife and it was uncomfortable for all of us.

My father would take me back to that avocado rental house on Sunday and after I moved away, my father and I didn't communicate very much at all.

Chapter 14: Kate

What I put that poor girl through all those years of my drunken madness is an ugliness that I will burden to redress entirely.

Our story has all the makings of a great screenplay only it is more incredulous being real in life.

The story started long ago at a grocery store. The grocery store was a niche store that offered an upscale shopping experience with full service parcel pick up and a giant fish tank guaranteeing freshness as the large fish were still swimming until packaged for delivery.

I was the fun guy who stocked the shelves and worked magic in the back room and Kate was the maestro at the front who tactfully handled all the needy customers. When she was returning something to the stockroom or the shelves or the freezer, we would sometimes run into each other.

We officially made a connection at an after work party hosted by a fellow stocker and then started seeing each other as a couple after that. At work, our blossoming romance was impossible to hide from the quacking hens of gossip central. I made the mistake of buying lovey dovey cards and flowers and items of romance right at the store. It really didn't matter to me and I paraded Kate around to show her off like a prize that I had won. The grand pageantry event was the store's annual Christmas party and it was a big deal. That year, it would take place around our six month anniversary and was being hosted at a fancy inn and conference center. The party had a disc jockey and some raffles and a nice dinner and free alcohol supposedly for legal agers only. Naturally, all company parties have some kind of drama, maybe someone gets too drunk or too amorous or too out of control.

The store's Christmas party was no exception and Kate and I scored some points with my antics. We got into a boisterous verbal argument fueled by my boozing and past jealousies. She managed to escape from me and I felt it my duty to go track her down. I went knocking on guest room doors where I thought secret work parties were being held and maybe with some boys and Kate is a pretty girl. All of the rooms whose doors I thumped on were occupied by regular inn guests and when I knocked on their door they screamed at me after I woke them up and scared them. I kept searching and thumping and making a scene and convincing people I was doing the right thing.

As an intoxicated gladiator, I felt justified trying to rescue young Kate from the horrors created in my head. The police were called and Kate was found unharmed. We explained it as a misunderstanding and I played the fool and ate crow. We both returned to work a couple days later and heard we made the hall of shame. Our story was far down the list and quickly got second billing. There were more trashy stories being circulated by the quacking hens of gossip central and our little story was too lame in comparison.

When we first started going out, Kate and I hung around her friends at garage parties and house parties. When we were not hanging out with her friends, we would spend time at my grandparent's house or her parent's house and go to dinner and on road trips and to state parks and those typical types of couple's things.

Kate knew I drank a lot sometimes but didn't know the full extent of my alcohol addiction with its hooks deeply embedded into my soul.

Naturally, I shared the addiction madness with like minded heavy drinking friends. Soon thereafter, I dragged poor Kate into these parties and into the empty chasm of industrial scale drinking with people who desired to get wasted as much as me. As the unsteady captain, I led Kate into the shallow ports of perpetual hollowness and dragged her down as the rudderless boat mindlessly floated to drunken events and the bars and the all night parties. I didn't see the emptiness in this lifestyle but Kate did and she had been aware of this for a long time and offered valuable insight. I ignored her insight and kept right on crashing that boat down the twisting river of alcohol abuse.

Somewhere in the catacombs of my consciousness, I thought it would be a great idea if Kate and I got married. My southern charm was a powerful weapon and hard to resist when creatively applied and we ended up getting married at the courthouse. About a year later, we were married in the church and it was a beautiful church and it was romantic and everything was headed for disaster. For years, my addiction train was close to derailing. After we got married, we moved to a little cottage on the lake and the velocity of the addiction train spiraled out of control and I went off the rails. Kate was stuck with me and alone at the cottage most of the time. I morphed into a bitter shell of a disturbed drunkard. With little hope of rescue, Kate managed to escape from the claws of my insanity. Looking back is difficult to this day. I was many shades of ugly. What I put that poor girl through all those years of my drunken madness is an ugliness that I will burden to redress entirely.

Fortunately, we both have moved past that and remain friends. For over twelve years, Kate has witnessed the sober version of me and I have witnessed her growth as a gifted writer and a talented singer and a great person. Per sempre forte.

Chapter 15: Wine Foot

A consistent thing early in my life was my relationship with alcohol. The relationship began as a third grader after I found a bottle of vermouth in the cupboard and drank it and discovered it helped to numb my emotions so I thought I had found a friend.

I didn't know exactly what was going on with my family but I knew something was wrong and the house was frighteningly quiet unless there was an alcohol fueled party going on in the basement. Even as a youngster, it wasn't difficult to find like minded kids who shared my penchant for the drink. Together, we would pool resources and liberate alcohol from our family and friends or find people willing to buy us some booze for a fee.

All of us troubled kids had some family issues and most of our families were heavy into drinking and siphoning alcohol from house parties was a breeze. Oftentimes, we were offered beers like one would pass a dinner roll. By the fifth grade, I was an active alcohol abuser and could handle my liquor as ridiculous as that sounds. Older kids liked to hang around me because I was smart and funny and charming and could drink a lot without causing too much drama.

Through the years, the pattern of drinking intensified and I drank more often and with harder liquor. From the sixth grade, I was drinking with the "big dogs." The big dogs moniker was how an older drinking buddy described the elite subset of mass boozers.

One night when he was drunk, this older drinking buddy drowned and he couldn't swim and it probably wouldn't have mattered anyway. Drowning while drunk was not completely uncommon in these parts and I was acquainted with another person who suffered the same fate.

Another older drinking buddy of mine had a unique mantra that he lived by: "If you buy beer before noon, you have to buy a case."

Well hell, early drinking offsets the misery of a hangover, so game on. The mantra became a call to arms and we bought all the beer and booze we could and drank until it was gone and then scrounged for more. For the most part, I liked "mantra man" and hung around him and his kids and his girlfriend often. Not surprisingly, he died young from alcohol related complications.

After I moved to the great Midwest, it didn't take long to find other circuses and parties and people to share the bottle for the purpose of getting drunk. There was one especially deranged circus that was most impressive with its vast scope and secluded venue.

This was the grand circus of human monkeys and I'll call this circus extravaganza Wine Foot. Wine Foot was an annual tradition that went back for years. Nobody was clear about its origins and nobody really cared either. The Wine Foot promoters marketed the extravaganza as a celebration of the return of the professional football season and it was now time to throw the hail mary to holy hell and maybe the devil could ride shotgun. The Wine Foot promoters enjoyed quick cash and happened to own some secluded property. The property was immense and had one big pond as its star attraction and several other smaller ponds as the supporting cast.

The property is large enough to easily accommodate the twenty plus vehicles scheduled to arrive. After entering the property, the vehicles will form a posse and encircle the large pond. The promoters of Wine Foot asked for seventy five dollars per vehicle. In exchange, they provided a couple kegs of beer and some snacks and some bug spray and unrestricted access to the property. Wine Foot promoters asked people to not leave the property until the morning to protect the promoters from the liability of being a party to the many drunk drivers under their purview. After every vehicle had arrived, the rickety gate to the property was shut. People could have easily moved the rickety gate and left at any point and nobody did. The vehicles that arrived were a mix of cars and trucks and campers. People brought tents and sleeping bags and trailers and blankets and lanterns and coolers and fishing poles and booze. Lots of booze.

My group of three brought some blankets and some pillows and some lanterns and some coolers and three cases of beer and four large plastic bottles of vodka and various mixer agents and cups and things like that. We had just one night to vanquish our competition and there were fierce competitors from heavy crew drunkards from all around the area. We had to represent.

There were about sixty people that showed up and many of us were eager to prove who the biggest baddest drinker was.

All of the guys were aware that the female combatants were skilled competitive drinkers too and the battle began. Like swarms of locusts, we all descended on the property and started drinking and walking around to exchange pleasantries and comparing coolers to see who the real players were and it was only the afternoon and there was a lot of drinking left. People spontaneously formed competitive sanctums with some people choosing more friendly areas of competition like bocce ball or horseshoes or just tossing the frisbee or the old football. The smart folks went fishing and swimming and grilled out and just chilled out and drank a little. Other people were far more serious and decided to play the game of shots and get right to it. Rookie mistake. Most of these folks doing the shots early on also passed out early.

As the afternoon moved into night, jaunting from one vehicle to the next was the thing to do. It was like bar hopping and meeting new groups of people and pretending to be cool and getting infinitely more wasted. There was a cacophony of lantern lights that added surrealism to the circus. I was about a bottle of vodka in before blacking out and my last memory was a battle of the band with people competing to show whose vehicle had the best sound system.

According to some people, I started to become aggressive and was challenging people to fight me. As the story was told, one of the frisbee tossers got me high and I mellowed out a little and then drank some more and then passed out in the open field.

Early the next morning, I woke up from my vodka coma still a bit drunk. I felt like a drunken pirate as one of my contacts was missing and my feet were naked and missing my giant flip flops. Instinctively, I knew my wallet was gone. After running around the property and the lakes, I managed to track down my flip flops and then bopped around like an intoxicated penguin.

All the party goers were packing it up and eventually the posse of vehicles slowly meandered out the open gate. To wrap up Wine Foot, all the party goers meet at a large restaurant for breakfast to say their goodbyes.

My traveling companions knew that my wallet was missing and that I had no money and they didn't offer to buy breakfast, so I stayed in the car.

That about sums it up for most drinking friends: when you need them, they're not there.

Chapter 16: Marble Head

After I moved to my grandparents, I visited that little southern town a few times. My first visit was surreal as I stayed in my old room at the avocado rental home. My room was frozen in time and everything was just like I left it.

My dresser still had some drawers left open and our family cat who loved me hung around all the time. The broken fish tank lay dormant and vintage stereo sat collecting dust. If I wasn't intoxicated, I would have experienced more of an emotional reaction.

I found some old friends and we did what we always do and we smoked some weed and drank a bunch of booze and reminisced. A few days later, I made the long drive back to my grandparents.

For the second visit, I brought along my great friend who I called Rotante in a previous chapter. Rotante was skeptical of the stories I had told him about growing up and came along to check it out for himself.

Rotante got his first taste of southern hospitality when a female party goer squatted down below him to do her business while he was doing his. Seemed like a great scheme to introduce herself as Rotante is a good looking guy. Rotante met some colorful characters when we hit the southern party scene.

He even got to see the avocado house where I grew up and there's a picture of us sitting on the porch and he's smiling. Rotante played the whole experience off as no big deal but I knew he was happy to leave.

Of the three visits, the final visit to the little southern town was the most bizarre. Vincent had a distant relative who had passed away and left him some money. Flush with cash, Vincent upgraded to a much nicer rental home and bought all new furnishings too.

The problem was that Vincent didn't have a reliable source of income and the inheritance money was spent in no time.

When I arrived, everything was in chaos. Vincent and mother had to move out by the end of the month or else they would be evicted. In a few weeks, they would have nowhere to live.

Vincent, however, didn't seem overly concerned about the situation. His plan was to move a state away to be closer to his daughter and then have his daughter find them a place to live.

So, Vincent and mother moved to the other state and his daughter found them a place to rent. The renting of the place went okay for a while but then the gremlin of rent no pay resurfaced and they needed a place to live again.

So, Vincent and mother moved in with Vincent's daughter and her family and the house was small and made smaller yet with their added baggage and human cargo.

Mother disliked not having much privacy and didn't like the hoards of people and disliked not having her own space and things began unraveling in her head or so it seemed.

During that period, mother called my grandmother frequently. My grandmother was kind and direct and wasn't keen on talking on the phone for too long and the phone was passed to me a lot.

So, I got to hear mother complain and she would describe the deteriorating home life situation and allude to her alleged deepening depression.

I was suspicious and cynical of anything mother purported happening to her. Mother played the victim well and she was good at it because she would convince herself and then it became factual to her. As the phone calls increased, mothers' mental state was made to sound disconnected.

Sometimes, mother seemed to be trying to sell my Grandmother or me on the idea that she was a mess.

On some level, mother probably was a mess but it was hard to separate the actual mess from the regular garbage. My opinion was that mother believed what she was saying to be true and the actual truth would always be a challenge to ascertain.

The calls from mother started arriving with increased frequency and intensity in the weeks to come.

Before he passed away, I was fortunate that I got to know my grandfather pretty well and we managed to get close. My grandfather wanted to spread joy and help bring a smile to people.

Part of my grandfather's strategy was to photocopy a cluster of comics that made the grade and then deliver this large comic packet to a lengthy list of friends and associates.

As his trusted staff of one, that is where I entered the picture. I was responsible for the administrative work and the delivery of the comics cluster. Out of respect, I always asked my grandfather who was doing the driving for the day and most times I did.

My grandfather was a kind hearted person who chose to see the good in people. He was always upbeat and positive and didn't let the stroke slow him down too much.

Besides the comics delivery avocation, he read all the time with no fewer than two dozen magazines and it seemed like he read them all in his favorite overstuffed chair.

It was near this chair where we would have our business meetings, usually concerning comic's selection and delivery priorities. My grandfather was sharp all the way to the end. He often said that all he wanted to do now was make it to his 50th wedding anniversary and he did.

The speech my grandfather gave during the anniversary celebration reminded everyone just what a powerhouse he was back in the day. Then, a short time later, my grandfather passed away. My grandfather's funeral procession was grand and he was remembered as a stalwart of the community.

After my grandfather passed away, it was just me and my grandmother in their house. My grandmother liked that I lived there and that she was not alone in the house. My grandmother was a kind person and from the era of confident stoicism and I rarely saw her emotionally charged one way or the other. My grandmother was self-sufficient and would do her own thing and she liked that I was around the house even if I sequestered myself in the den or the basement. To my chagrin, my grandma drove a sportier car than me, so I tried to borrow it as often as I could. My grandma drove herself around town and I would drive her out of town and out of state to visit friends and family.

My grandmother was a kind person with a quiet wisdom and we got a little closer. I respected her gentle manner and her genuineness and her great sense of humor. During her milestone surprise birthday party, my grandmother made it her mission to say hello to everybody who attended in her honor and she did and there were a lot of people.

My grandmother was a class act who practiced turning the other cheek and helping others in need. She helped neighbors and friends and family and total strangers. She even helped Vincent and mother on a few occasions.

A few months after the phone calls from mother started, Vincent called my grandmother to report that he was driving mother up soon and that maybe mother should stay there for awhile. Vincent said that mother was struggling and he didn't know what else to do. Vincent was quite resourceful when he wanted to be and his story was full of holes from the start. With the saga of mother and Vincent though, a shoddy screenplay was a common feature. A few weeks later, Vincent shows up with mother and they both enter through the garage. When I first saw mother, she looked disheveled and her clothes looked really dirty. My first thought was why did Vincent allow her to wear these dirty clothes and make her entrance this way. Despite my animosity towards mother, I still loved her on some level and didn't like seeing her like this. My senses detected deception principally with Vincent. Mother walked with an unsteady gait and seemed to be scanning the house looking for other occupants. When mother spoke, her voice sounded like speech augmented with some type of added quiver either for effect or totally innate. Something was not right. That part would be difficult to determine with both mother and Vincent on the same script. Mother didn't say very much and then walked back to the den and layed down.

This bizarre entrance made my grandmother noticeably uncomfortable and I wanted to diffuse it by gnawing on some small talk with Vincent. Small talk should have been simple for Vincent. He had experience in sales and small talk is a fundamental tool. Holy hell, even when Vincent was a few weeks from being evicted during my last trip there, he was prattling on with all sorts of ridiculous small talk all while barbecuing and shoveling down beers.

Now at my grandmother's house, Vincent was pretentious and wouldn't break the ice with simple small talk. When Vincent chose to not get off script, I knew he was playing us on some level. Vincent said he was staying at a motel and thought it would be best if mother stayed there with my grandmother. On his way out the door, Vincent told my grandmother that it was by the grace of god that mother is alive and that she tried to open the truck door while motoring down the highway and he pulled her back just in time.

After Vincent closed the door and got back into his truck, I told my grandmother that I didn't think Vincent's story was truthful and my grandmother agreed. In my private thoughts, however, I thought Vincent was full of crap and was attempting to use my grandmother's religious convictions to bolster his credibility.

I don't remember Vincent ever talking about religion or god or anything related to the bible except when cursing at his bad fortune, usually when he was drinking. Vincent oversold the story and that was a rookie mistake for a skilled salesman like him.

A few days later, Vincent left alone and returned home to live with his daughter.

For the next week, mother slept often. I suspected much of that had to do with the fact that she and Vincent had unofficially separated a casualty of the now long distance relationship. Whatever you call what they had together, they had it a long time. I believe mother derailed a little when she realized it was a no win situation for her: stay with Vincent and be miserable living with his daughter's family or move in with my grandmother and have a nice place but no Vincent. After living with grandmother for about a month, however, mother seemed to improve significantly. Mother took over my grandfather's old room and it soon resembled a teenager's room with band posters on the wall and a portable boombox.

From time to time, Vincent would make the long drive to visit mother. They would spend time together and invite people over to my grandmother's house for the barbecue and the many drinks. During these barbecues, it was particularly difficult for me to play nice and to see the two of them together like nothing happened. In the catacomb of my soul, I saw both of them as scoundrels for pulling me into their vortex of abject ugliness.

In my eyes, mother was the principal scoundrel and Vincent was the vagabond boyfriend. Nonetheless,

Vincent was a likable guy and was smooth and charming and it was easy for people to enjoy the barbecue and smile for the pictures.

At one point, Vincent decided to move out of his daughter's house and to relocate thousands of miles away. Now that Vincent lived so far away from mother, the only practical way they could see each other was by taking an airplane. Since Vincent claimed he was afraid to fly, that burden of flying would fall to mother.

So now, my grandmother and mother and I all share the same house. From my account, it seemed that mother's emotional development had retrograded and from what I witnessed, it appeared that mother didn't respect my grandmother's house that much either.

As the years progressed, things got more difficult for my grandmother. It looked like mother continued on as an adult teenager in the emotional development sphere. For my aging grandmother, having a teenage version of an adult daughter was not ideal for the role of caregiver.

Before any of this played out, however, I moved out of my grandmother's house. I had to get away from mother before the relationship between us got more toxic. There were too many unresolved issues and the issues never did get resolved.

Chapter 17: Carnival

When I moved to my grandparents, I was already a little bit messed up from some childhood experiences and by my own doing later on. From outside appearances, I was upbeat and optimistic. I was a people pleaser and wanted people to like me and being friendly was important in that regard. I thought I had adequately buried most of my darkness but sometimes people saw a burst of rage and those episodes freaked people out. Alcohol seemed to quell the dark emotions but sometimes too much of the hard stuff had the opposite effect.

When I moved to my grandparents, I didn't know anyone in the city. My grandparents and I were effectively strangers and it was awkward for all of us. I borrowed my grandmother's cool little sporty car and drove around places like the park looking for friends.

During that period, my appetite for booze had steadily increased. I had packed several large plastic jugs of vodka in my suitcase and despite being underage buying more booze was a breeze.

The cycle continued for a while and then I found work doing odd jobs and then some factory jobs. In the factories, the cast of characters were similar to the folks I had known in the little southern town plus the drinking game was the same no matter where you went. By then, I drank the hard stuff and finding someone who shared my proclivities for industrial drinking required little effort.

At different moments of time, I had the pleasure of meeting many talented ringmasters. In the addiction carnival, the skilled ringmaster craftily guides the attendees through the empty chasm of alcohol abuse. I had the fortune of meeting two hall of fame ringmasters who I will call Corto and Parlare.

I met Corto after I started working for an outreach organization. Corto was charming and had a magnetic personality that drew people to him. Some people were impressed with his credentials and seemingly impressive accomplishments. As an organization inspired by a powerful mantra, people from the same circle came to admire Corto.

As I soon discovered, however, Corto was a mess with many areas of his own life and he tried to keep that hidden. Corto and I started the free fall of holiday addiction during the organization's annual Christmas party. That night, Corto was the master of ceremonies. When he was at the podium, he gave a rambling speech and was noticeably intoxicated. I thought it was a foolhardy move as he gave the intoxicated speech in front of shallow guests. After the party, he invited me over to his house with a couple of select staff members and I should have known better.

At that point, I had been sober for a little over a year. At the after party, I had a glass of beer and that's all it took to start my descent back into full time drinking. After that night, I went over to Corto's house on several occasions. Corto wined and dined me and grilled filet steaks and created powerful alcoholic drinks to indulge before and after dinner. Before long, I was firmly planted in the heavy drinking carnival. Corto poured attention on me and made me feel special like his best friend and trusted advisor. Corto pulled out all stops and even gained access to a large boat. We floated around and drank fine whiskey with fancy glasses and listened to party music with parrots symbolically sitting on our shoulders. Kate warned me that Corto was not a real friend and that he would use me until he found somebody else. Of course, I didn't listen to her. I was convinced that Corto and I were genuine friends and that we were connected on some level. It finally dawned on me that everything Corto and I did revolved around the carnival of alcohol abuse and I was the star attraction. After I resigned for a different job, Corto stopped contacting me all together and had moved on to the next clown.

This final hall of fame ringmaster had a much longer tenure than Corto. I will call him Parlare. I met Parlare when he started working as a member of my team and I was his boss. I didn't take supervising too seriously most of the time and tried to keep it as entertaining as possible. These particular positions demanded physical toughness and were not easy to fill. I liked Parlare right away. He seemed to skip in the work room and possessed an upbeat persona with great energy. Parlare and his wife and family lived in an apartment down the road from the store. I often gave Parlare a ride home from work and he would offer drinks and I accepted naturally. We both would drink a lot and I was surprised that he could drink as much as me and we had drinks frequently. We started hanging around each other outside of work too. Oftentimes, we included his wife and other friends and me. All of the functions were fueled by lots of booze and we drank heavy crew style. Parlare was always the star of the show and nobody ever objected.

He was fun and kept everyone entertained with eloquently told stories and far fetched fables and wild antics. I was introduced to Parlare's extended family and we all shared an affinity for the drink and for wild parties. Parlare was exceptional as the group leader and his specialty was large group drinking events. Even the parties held at Parlare's modest dwellings were elaborate events for family and the select friends in attendance. Parlare got highly energized from having the spotlight raining down on him and rain it did. These parties always involved many different types of alcohol and the booze factor became a competition as to who would bring the most exotic hootch.

Booze fueled other competitive avenues like football and basketball and volleyball and drinking games. In addition, Parlare was fearless in collecting souls for his crock pot of debauchery and hedonism. One example I witnessed first hand was when we went to an outdoor concert together. Parlare interjected himself into a large group of girls and then started groping them openly with seemingly little resistance. Parlare then helped the girls get on stage with intimate levels of physical exploration and naughtiness. Parlare thought of himself as a player and the inconvenience of marriage didn't slow him down.

For me, the fact that Parlare and I went back years was a sign of a genuine friendship. When we did get together, Parlare's enthusiasm further sold me and maybe he wasn't trying to sell me at all. Even when Parlare propositioned Kate for indecency, I didn't completely sever ties. I told myself that Parlare is a dog and this is what a dog does and he was denied anyway poor guy. In all the years we hung out, the time was spent drinking at some function. Perhaps, drinking was the only glue that truly connected us and I still miss him despite it all.

After being sober for twelve years, I still wonder if there was ever anything genuine between us. I like to think so, and I try not to delude myself, but yet I wonder.

Chapter 18: Discarded Darkness

With mother now living with my grandmother, I suspected that my grandmother would be challenged and that my grandmother would get the worst end of the deal down the road. I respected my grandmother and had a sense of duty to protect her. Nevertheless, my grandmother was aware of mother's foibles and unique challenges. Mother and Vincent asked many favors of my grandmother through the years and my classy grandmother would usually oblige.

Additionally, at one point, I drove my grandmother down south in her sporty car. My grandmother wanted to see for herself how mother lived, so we visited mother and Vincent in that wretched little rental house. My grandmother also got to see my sad little room upstairs that was still frozen in time. I could tell that my grandmother was disturbed at what she saw. My grandmother, however, never judged mother and we left a few days later.

When I was living with my grandparents, I was a mess and moved gradually deeper into darkness. I kept that mess buried most of the time. People usually saw this optimistic and friendly young guy who was caring and helpful.

That was also a part of me and I helped my grandparents and other people too. Except for the times when I pissed the couch, my drinking didn't overflow my internal levee system and flood the banks of my grandparent's lives.

After mother moved in with my grandmother, I knew that I had to get away from her. Our relationship was already toxic and it would just get worse if we lived together. In a clandestine manner, I went apartment hunting and I didn't want mother to catch wind of the plan. I felt guilty that I was leaving my grandmother and angry at mother for upending both of our lives. Soon after, I found an apartment and moved out.

My direction in life was far from stationary and I worked in many different occupational fields. Along the way, my combustion engine was building pressure as I pushed myself to drink harder and faster to pass out quicker to get some sleep for work. Drinking was the most important part of my life and working was just a means to keep that going.

At work, some people made comments about my hangover haze and occasional alcohol stench. I adapted quickly to quash the alcohol stench and used a powerful charcoal body wash that made some people sneeze.

It didn't matter which occupational arena I was competing in as drinking always came first. After work, I often went to bars and then home to finish drinking and then to eat and then to sleep.

Other times, I would take drinking baths. I had a terrible habit of drinking while I was in the bathtub full of bubbles. Before I would get in the bathtub, I would get half drunk and then finish the job while floating and listening to music and drinking. More than a few times, I passed out in the bathtub and woke up not quite submerged but close. I vowed to be more careful next time and I was until it happened again. The last time it was a close call and I woke up partially submerged and that really freaked me out, so I stopped taking drunken baths after that.

In its place, I took extended sit down showers and kind of kicked back and listened to some music and drank some vodka from a plastic bottle and those showers became a ritual for years.

A few times to be closer to work, I moved some distance from my grandparents home base. It didn't matter where I lived as I just kept sliding down the ramp of darkness. It was at one of these exits where I got busted for drunk driving.

Kate and I attended an all day drunk festival and it was now well past midnight. Even though Katie was sober, I insisted on driving. I was speeding down a frontage road and drove right past an officer and was arrested for drunk driving.

At the post drunk driving alcohol assessment a few weeks later, I lied my way through it and convinced the alcohol counselor that I was a social drinker and this was a one off. This was so far from the reality of my life during that time.

I didn't think that I could ever stop drinking. At that stage in my life, I had tried to stop drinking and moderate it on many occasions. The moderation part never worked for me. If there was any booze in my dwelling, I would have to drink it until it was gone. I tried the stop drinking path too with limited success. I was never sober for more than a year with the sober period typically a month or two.

At most of my occupations, I was a functioning drunk with some jobs just barely functional. With the chronic hangovers and the many intoxicated morning commutes to work, I was never operating at full capacity.

It was getting more challenging to conceal my inner darkness, so I drank more to bury the emotions.

Sometimes though, I got beyond earthly drunk and had to go to the emergency room. It was quite serious a couple of times with one time in particular nearly lethal. Somehow, I made it to the emergency room. I was far from lucid but mainly intelligible.

From what I was told, my blood alcohol level was over forty percent and it's lucky I was not in a coma or dead. I was fortunate as they kept me alive and safe as I worked through the extended detox.

After detox, I was entered into the locked ward of inpatient treatment and inpatient treatment at this hospital was good. We were treated well and the treatment regime was solid with many classes being taught in a wide range of disciplines like psychology and art therapy and substance abuse. I completed the program and managed to stay sober for a while.

After I started drinking heavily again, I became unstable. Long before, I had landed at an upper house apartment and it was within walking distance of all the bars. I had started to drink as often as I could and found myself in some dangerous situations.

At some point, I had lost my job and managed to protract the rent but went without power for two years. I used a battery powered light and ate canned foods and it was all pathetic and sad, so I drank more.

At one point, I was transported to the county for alcohol inpatient treatment. If you didn't have much money or insurance, this is where you got sent.

The beaten facility at the county was terrifying at times and the doctor of the ward was openly aggressive and seemed hateful of drunkards like me.

The ward had souls with many ailments and no clear criteria of who goes where or any clear strategy to help the people who were struggling.

It looked like everybody was just being warehoused with the more fortunate folks just waiting out a mandatory holding period. For the mass of souls on the ward, there was really nothing to do but vegetate and linger. Food was presented on a large tray on a recreation table. The food just sat there much of the day until it was restocked.

My name was called the following afternoon and they told me to go. After passing through a couple of security doors, I was let outside and that was it.

Then, I walked back to my house apartment and that's where the story picks up later.

Chapter 19: Roles & Scripts

Each of us plays many roles and every role has its own individual script. One of our longest lasting roles is that of an employee. Many occupations have their own job description and the script is spelled out in detail.

One can view the job title as the role and the job description as the script.

Some job titles don't need a job description. An example is a lawyer. Most people have a basic understanding of what they think a lawyer does.

Our lifetime role of working is clear cut. If we don't please our employer most of the time, we won't be working. Our employer has rules we are supposed to follow and goals we are supposed to meet. In exchange for our lifetime of servitude, we are compensated with a paycheck and some benefits hopefully.

Contrast the employee role with the lifelong role in our family. Family roles and scripts are rarely clear cut. In most families, the primary roles are more or less defined by titles.

We typically have the primary roles of mother & father and son & daughter. Each individual in the family thinks they know what the other role is supposed to be doing but there isn't something like a template for families to use.

Everyone has their own take on what a mother & father and son & daughter ought to be doing but nobody is using the same script.

For the kids, the role dynamic is made even more dramatic when the principal role of son & daughter is subdivided. Let me give you some examples.

In the first example, one of the sons is a good listener, so everybody in the family takes advantage of his listening skills. With no human involvement, this son is transplanted into the role of family counselor and is now expected to listen to people's problems. This son didn't choose the role but is now expected to perform the function. Each person in the family uses this son, the family counselor, as they see fit.

In the second example, the daughter is a popular high school student. The daughter is doing well and has many friends and many social activities.

Behind the scenes, however, the family is a mess and needs a distraction. Better yet, it wants a hero.

So guess what, the daughter is transplanted into the role of the family hero. The family uses the hero to deceive and give the impression that everything is okay. Everything is not okay.

The family wants people to take notice of how well the daughter is doing, thereby proving that the family is just fine. The family is not fine.

Like the son, there is no human involvement in the transplant process and the daughter is now the family hero. The family hero has constant pressure to continue performing at a high level. If the family hero falters, the family's secrets will be betrayed. The family wants to avoid that at all costs.

In the final example, the other son is getting into trouble and acting out. The acting out is just a reflection of what's really happening in the family. Behind the curtain, the family is a big mess.

Most people in the family play along and pretend that everything's okay but the other son refuses to play along and acts out. This acting out brings much unwanted attention to the family, so the other son is transplanted into the scapegoat role and blamed for the family's problems.

The roles shown in the previous examples are not unique and occur in families of every socioeconomic status. Some roles are transplanted into individuals without consent and the recipient of the role now has to execute it. People lose a part of their identity with each transplanted role and become a piece of the family puzzle.

Imagine a simple wooden jigsaw puzzle for kids ages four to eight. You know the one that has a tray with the reference picture for the twelve easy puzzle pieces. In the case of my family, the jigsaw puzzle was originally five pieces. On the following page, the transplanted roles are filled in the parentheses.

1. mother
2. father
3. older brother (family hero role)
4. sister (scapegoat role)
5. me (quiet child role)

As the family hero, my older brother brought a veneer of respectability to the mess that was our family.

My sister was transplanted into the horrible role of scapegoat. My sister was acting out all the family's issues and was taking a beating for it.

My sister and mother fought and traded punches and pulled each other's hair out. It was terrifying to witness and I didn't know what to think.

In the early years, I was a quiet kid but that all changed later. After mother moved in with my grandmother, family members from down south would come and visit. When we were all together, it was painfully awkward for all of us, so the clown was born.

The clown was able to diffuse the awkwardness rapidly. When I was drinking the heavy stuff, the clown got out of control sometimes. Other than to say that I drank too much, family members seldom criticized the clown. When the clown was chastised for drinking, I would tell them to get with the giddy up and keep up with me and that I didn't get drunk all by myself.

The clown played an important role and allowed people to forget about the family mess and drink freely and enjoy the show.

After my father totally checked out, his piece of the puzzle was gone. Now, the puzzle was down to four pieces. Not long after moving in with my grandmother, mother morphed into something I called the adult child.

1. mother (adult child role)
2. older brother (family hero role)
3. sister (scapegoat role)
4. me (now the clown role)

After I chose to get sober, the clown jigsaw piece was removed from an already unstable family puzzle. There was no longer the clown to help diffuse the messy family dynamics. The family hero had burned out trying to save the family and the scapegoat had little purpose now and the family splintered again.

Before I understood family systems, I thought that my sobriety would help improve the situation for my family collectively. As far as the family puzzle was concerned, it made things far worse.

The clown was vital in helping people forget about the mess that was surrounding them. At least initially, I suspect that people would have welcomed the relief that the clown could have brought back to the family.

Back in the day, drinking stories involving me were sometimes regaled.

- **Family**: “Remember all your empty vodka bottles under the couch?”

- **Me**: “You realize that I haven’t drank in years.”

- **Family**: “Come on man. Just reliving the good old days.”

- **Me**: “How about when I got so drunk I ended up in the hospital?”

I suspect these stories were told to try and get under my skin. The attempt at shaming has more to do with the people telling the story than with me. I gave my monkey the boot and made changes in my life and sometimes change is not welcome. Don’t expect others to change just because you are changing. If people are remotely content with their own lives, they won’t want to change. Regardless of who is doing the changing, other people will resist it. I suspect that people sometimes miss the drunken clown. In the family puzzle, the drunken clown was a big piece of the puzzle and that piece is now gone. Through the years, I have felt different versions of sabotage. I believe the sabotage is generated more at a subconscious level and I don't believe most of the sabotage is deliberate.

People just want things to be like they were before, back in the good old days. Be aware that sabotage is likely to happen and be prepared for it. If you understand what's happening, it won't be an issue.

I recommend taking inventory of your own roles. Were these roles freely accepted or chosen? Keep in mind that some roles go all the way back to your childhood. With some roles being a part of us for so long, they may seem natural. Some roles have been transplanted into us and have taken a life of their own. It's your right to keep the roles, update them as you see fit, make amends to them, cancel them entirely or whatever you wish.

Chapter 20: Forgiveness

Through the years, the dynamic between mother and my grandmother shifted. Before I got pulled into the vortex of alcohol abuse, I would visit my grandmother's house regularly. When I was there, I could see the writing on the wall.

My grandmother started to need a little more assistance and with mother being an adult child, she was not particularly helpful. Assistance for my grandmother was arranged and she received help from home health workers.

While my grandmother was being helped, mother learned that being needy brought her attention too. I don't believe mother made up all her ailments. I believe she had convinced herself of the symptoms and that is how they were reported to the doctors.

Soon thereafter, both my grandmother and mother were being assisted by a steady stream of health care workers. In the months to come, they both received increased layers of home health care until my grandmother passed away. After my grandmother passed away, the house was sold. After that, mother needed a place to live and we found her an apartment and I helped her move in. After mother moved into the apartment, much of the family tried to help her maintain a more independent lifestyle.

Mother resisted it from the start and the push back continued through the years. I believe mother was still looking for someone to take care of her like my grandfather took care of my grandmother. Over time, the continuation of mother's saga grew in intensity with a chain of events ultimately leading to tragedy.

After years of playing the needy card, it all came crashing down and mother ended up in a nursing home. One day, she was rushed to the emergency room. Throughout the years, mother had been rushed to the emergency room many times.

Every time, she would stay at the hospital for a short period of time and then be sent home mainly recovered. This trip to the emergency room didn't seem any different but tragically it was.

Ultimately, mother's medical power of attorney decided to allow her to pass away and everybody agreed it was for the best.

Nobody explained that a person's passing can last for days and it did. The process was grotesque and seemed inhumane to me. It shattered my heart to see her like that. To this day, that experience has made me more sensitive to the suffering of others.

My relationship with mother was complicated. Despite our history, I still loved her. During the final days, I told her that I loved her and that I forgave her.

Forgiving someone may be viewed as disentangling yourself from a strong emotional hold that binds you to them. By disentangling yourself, it can help set you free. Let me give you an example.

I’m sure you have heard someone say something like this before, “I’ll never forgive them for what they did. Not in a million years.” Not forgiving this person doesn’t affect them in the least. Why would it?

They didn’t care then.
Why would they care now?

By forgiving the person, you take back power by disentangling your emotions from them. It may feel counterintuitive but it works. If it helps, call it disentangling.

To conclude this chapter, let’s talk about something that sounds easy to do: saying you're sorry. In practice, however, you may find it more difficult than you think. As human beings, we are going to mess up all the time. That’s just part of the deal. This is particularly true with the people we are close to.

For whatever reason, people don’t like to admit when they are wrong even if they are wrong. It probably has something to do with the ego as explained by psychoanalytic theories and other schools of thought.

Just think back to the last time you messed up with your loved one. Was your first thought to say I’m sorry? It wasn’t my first thought either.

I believe people want to justify why they do the things they do and then trap themselves by defending their justification. For all of our faults, human beings are forgiving creatures. When the person who wronged us apologizes and asks for forgiveness, we typically do.

From my own experience, it takes a lot of practice to get in the habit of saying I'm sorry.

Chapter 21: Hot Potato

Everybody is uniquely flawed one way or another. After all, we're only human beings. Even the most enlightened person in the world has some kind of issue. People usually have some part of themself they may not like and may not want to accept and may not even recognize. Much of this takes place at a subconscious level and is buried in the basement of our brain. I will refer to this subconscious burial as a person's shadow side as referenced by Carl Jung.

A great way to gain insight into your shadow side is to explore your pet peeves. Discovering what you don't like in other people is usually telling of what you don't like about yourself.

Exploring our pet peeves may help to provide an illuminating window into our psyche. By paying attention to our pet peeves, we can learn a lot by examining them.

I will use myself as an example. Listed below are some of my pet peeves.

1. Soft spoken people
2. People who are too friendly
3. Plastic people

Let me start with the soft spoken pet peeve. In the beginning, the person I thought I was annoyed with is a friend who is soft spoken at times. After some digging, I discovered that the person I am actually annoyed with is myself.

Sometimes, I can be hard to understand when I talk quietly and sort of mutter to myself. I usually do this when I can't find the right word and my brain grinds to a crawl with all the mental tabs left open. It frustrates me because I like to think that I am on top of my game all the time. Of course, I'm not on top of my game all the time, I'm only human. I have to accept what seems obvious now and learn to be more patient with myself and others too.

Next on the pet peeve list is people who are too friendly. On the surface, the pet peeve sounds petty. I try not to judge the pet peeve and just allow myself to just examine it. I was at a large grocery store the other day and made contact with an uber friendly store associate. I found myself wanting to yell at this person and tell them to take it down a notch. Of course, I didn't do that and remained pleasant.

It dawned on me that this friendly store associate was similar in style to my personality during my working hours. I got annoyed with this friendly store associate because I annoy myself sometimes. I discovered when I pretend to be happy and friendly when I'm not really feeling it, I envision myself slithering down a pretentious slide and that scares me. This fear of being pretentious aligns well with my next pet peeve.

The final pet peeve on the list is people who are plastic. A wonderful example of this plasticity comes from a golden couple in the extended family. Every Christmas, the golden couple mails out a mass shipment of picture cards.

The Christmas picture cards are custom made and feature the golden couple standing in front of their beautiful home. In the picture, the golden couple is surrounded by their lovely children and the family dog and the nanny to pay homage to all the little helpers.

In the Christmas picture, everyone is looking the part of the dandy. Even the dog is wearing his Sunday best. The Christmas picture card omits nonessentials like Jesus and Santa.

It's possible that Santa and Jesus are staying in the guest house just in case they are summoned.

When I thought more about the golden couple, I discovered some interesting insights. What difference is it to me how the golden couple choose to live their lives? I should probably focus more on my own life.

While I have little in common with the golden couple, I'm still a bit plastic myself. I use face creams and hair products to keep myself looking pretty. With my lifestyle devoid of alcohol and smoking, I strike a pose of a good looking guy and that pleases me. I am learning to accept the plastic part of myself and other people too.

Let's continue forward and talk more about our thoughts. Our own thoughts are extraordinarily powerful. We talk to ourselves all the time. It's called self-talk.

We have thousands of thoughts every day and many of our thoughts are negative. The critical voice in our head affects how we feel and subsequently how we act.

Envision all the negative thoughts that have been festering in our head throughout the years. It's likely that these negative thoughts have not been challenged.

The negative thoughts have gained momentum and some have become a permanent recording. Some negative thoughts are particularly vile and we work hard to get rid of them quickly. I will share two of my most vile thoughts below.

- "I'm a failure."
- "I wasted my life."

These are some horribly vile thoughts. The thoughts can surface anytime and are more frequent during periods of heavy stress. These heavyweight negative thoughts are what I call "hot potato thoughts."

Picture a giant potato that just finished cooking in the oven. Now imagine that we forgot to use an oven mitt and then grab the hot potato right from the oven. We soon discover that the potato is painfully hot and we toss it from one hand to the other to avoid getting burnt.

It's a similar scene when these hot potato thoughts surface in our head. Hot potato thoughts are so vile that we want to get rid of them quickly. We then pass the hot potato to other people who are connected to us in some way. Passing the hot potato is far more egregious than having a bad day and taking it out on someone. These hot potato thoughts are the most negative thoughts we have and these vile thoughts have been allowed to fester like emotional black mold.

I will use one of my most vile hot potato thoughts, "I'm a failure." In the example that follows, Vincent stopped over to watch some football.

1. My hot potato thought: ***"I'm a failure."***
2. Me passing the hot potato: ***"Vincent, why didn't you ever finish college? You were only a semester away."***

See how I passed my hot potato onto Vincent. For now, I feel a little better about myself. Later, I will feel guilty about being a jerk to Vincent. The feeling of guilt will feed the "I'm a failure" thought monster and it will continue to gain momentum. In the process of passing the hot potato, I made Vincent feel bad and probably incited his hot potato thought monster too. Hot potato thoughts will continue to be a long time monster. Unless the thoughts are challenged, the cycle will continue.

Be aware that other people are passing their own hot potatoes onto you. If you're comfortable doing so, call them on it and explain what you think is happening. Keep in mind that other people are not going to talk about these types of thoughts. You will need to open up first to show them it's okay to talk about it.

- **Me**: "Vincent, I sometimes have thoughts that I'm a failure."

- **Vincent**: "Oh come on man, you're okay. Turn on the game."

- **Me**: "I'm serious Vincent. Let me share what I learned."

There is a book that can help. The book talks about Cognitive Behavioral Therapy (CBT). Cognitive Behavioral Therapy will help challenge negative thoughts. The book is called "Feeling Good: The New Mood Therapy" by David D. Burns.

Chapter 22: Recordings & Learned Behavior

Do we ever really think about what to do when we're at a stop light? How about talking to strangers? What about a woman's place? How about looking both ways before crossing the street? How about winning at all costs? Some thoughts and ideas get burned in our brain and become automatic like a recording. Some of the concepts of recordings come from the study of social interactions led by Eric Berne. Eric Berne is a 20th century psychiatrist who developed the theory of transactional analysis.

In the analysis, much of our thought processes may be viewed as a recording and many of these recordings become automatic. The recordings are essentially carried over from our childhood. The thoughts and ideas are fed to us very early in life and feature many "should" and "ought" and "must" and "don't."

When we need to take immediate action, some automatic thoughts are important. Let me provide a couple of examples. In the first example, imagine you are driving in your car when a guy on a bicycle darts right in front of you. Luckily for the bicyclist, I avoided hitting him. It's nearly instant from the moment of the automatic thought, “**STOP**,” to the actual slamming of the brakes.

In the second example, we invite a good friend over for a barbecue and she brings along her young son. The little kid is just having fun and jumping around and is about to stumble into a large fire pit. We all scream, “**LOOK OUT**,” and instantly bolt like a pack of cheetahs and tackle the kid and save the day. As you can tell from the examples, some thought recordings are important for safety. Most automatic thoughts, however, are not important for survival. Yet, these other thought recordings continue to influence our lives. Let me give you an example.

Imagine you are driving down the road and see a person of a different race and your first thought is something negative. That thought is not anything we’re born with and is one of many similar types of thoughts burned into our brain.

We have all sorts of negative thoughts and the thoughts may center around people from different backgrounds or people from different educational arenas or how people dress or where people live or what church people attend or where their kids go to school or what people eat or what kind of car people drive and so on. Literally, we have hundreds of recordings saved in our head.

Where do all of these recordings come from?

All of the recordings are composed of ideas and attitudes that we copy from people who we consider authority figures. The authority figures can include our parents, teachers, aunts and uncles, grandparents, older siblings, family friends, social media, politicians, and so on.

Our chosen authority figure may not be the best source of information. Keep in mind that our authority figures also received information from their own authority figures and so on through the generations. Who knows, maybe the origin of much of the information had some flaws right from the start.

With that in mind, take inventory of your thought recordings. Try to recognize the thought recordings as ideas and beliefs that have been a part of us for a long time. It's likely that many thought recordings are composed of attitudes and ideas that we copied from other people.

That's not to say that all of what we copied is good or bad. It just may not be our own. We have the power to rewrite our own script and choose beliefs and ideas that are in harmony with who we are today.

Now, let's turn our attention to the concept of learned behavior. Before we do that, however, let's talk about what has become the prevailing model of alcohol treatment.

The model is sometimes called the disease model.

The disease model describes an addiction as a disease with genetic, neurological and biological sources as the origin.

One of the goals of the disease model is to minimize the stigma sometimes associated with being an alcohol or drug abuser. The model implies that the addicted person has a disease and is not necessarily a bad person. Some people believe that a version of the disease model was first introduced to help returning veterans. Many returning veterans were impacted by drugs and alcohol or turned to drugs and alcohol to help cope with their experience. Back in the early days, a drunkard was seen as a weak person who lacked morals and character. A therapeutic tool like the disease model was useful because it helped to minimize the stigma associated with being an alcohol or drug abuser.

The disease model offered an alternative interpretation of drug addicted people as individuals who are sick and suffering from a disease and are not necessarily bad people who lack morals or character.

Fast forward to today.

In human service organizations, the disease model of addiction treatment is prevalent. Many human service organizations subscribe to the mantra of "alcoholism is a disease" or something similar in scope. There has always been debate about the validity of the disease model.

I have been on both sides of the alcohol coin: as an alcohol abuser receiving help and as an alcohol counselor providing assistance. As an alcohol counselor, it didn't matter to me if my employer subscribed to any particular addiction model and it definitely didn't matter when I was receiving help.

Now, let's return to the concept of learned behavior.

In the 1970's, the idea of social learning was put into theory by psychologist Albert Bandura. The theory is easy to understand. It's based on the notion that people can learn from each other through observation, imitation and modeling. In essence, we learn behavior from others.

My own life experience leans more toward the learned behavior model than the disease model of addiction. That's not to say that genetic traits didn't play some part for me.

By social learning, I modeled drinking behavior and started drinking early in life. I learned that it was acceptable to drink and alcohol abuse was a normal part of my life. Everybody I knew drank: my parents and my siblings and my circle of friends and their parents and so on. All the adults I knew accepted drinking parties. In fact, some of the most wild parties were hosted by the so-called adults. All of this chaos reinforced alcohol abuse as normal behavior. In my world, the prevailing attitude about alcohol abuse was chronic indifference.

In terms of attitudes and behavior, we learn a great deal from others. We likely learn some good and some bad with the rest somewhere in between. With that in mind, take time to review what I call the "family playbook."

The family playbook contains all the thought recordings and all of the rules of learned behavior. The good news is that we can learn new ways to do things and the thought recordings can be effectively challenged.

There is a book that can help. The book is called "I'm OK - You're OK" by Thomas Harris. The book talks about Transactional Analysis. Thomas Harris believes that by exploring the structure of our personalities and understanding old decisions, we can find the freedom to change our lives.

Chapter 23: Pretty Boy

After being released from the county for inpatient treatment, I walked back to my house apartment. As soon as I returned, I started drinking right away as I had a jug of vodka in the shower and that's all it took to reignite me. I looked around this vast empty space and wondered how I got here in the first place. It was years ago when I first saw an ad to lease the second story of a large house and I called to schedule a time to meet with the owner.

Before meeting the owner, I got myself all prettied up. When we met for the first time, the homeowner had a little twinkle in his eye and seemed attracted to me. I had seen that twinkle before with other guys and I didn't share the twinkle but it didn't matter and I used it to my advantage. I never let on that I was not into him and thought he was fake and oily. I skillfully swatted at his glittering ball of yarn and signed the lease and moved in a couple days later.

The second floor house apartment was vast. It had a big living room, two large bedrooms, a dining room, a spacious kitchen, a nice bathroom and a back patio. It also had access to a small third floor that looked like it was used for some form of homeschooling and even had some small desks.

When I was drunk, I would go up to the third floor and smoke some weed. A couple of times when I was up there, I thought I could hear kids saying something to me and I couldn't understand what they were saying and it seemed like they were messing with me and it freaked me out. I had experiences like that before at the abandoned resort and I tried to discount all those experiences as creations of a drug addled mind.

For furnishing the apartment, I had a loveseat, some pillows, a few blankets, a small table, a large boombox, and some clothes and that was about it.

So, like a rock star in a mansion, I secluded myself into one room with the rest of the place kept mostly empty and the one room was my home for the next few years. For a drunkard like me, however, the house apartment was perfect as it was located close to all the bar life the city had on tap.

Most of the bars that I went to didn't care how drunk you got as long as you had some money and could walk out on your own power. I sometimes got so drunk at the bars, it would take me an hour to maneuver the key into the lock of the house.

One time when nobody was home, a burglar broke into the house and stole some computer equipment from the first floor office and some of my clothes from my second floor apartment.

When I first started living in the house apartment, I was working at a large telecommunications company as a commissioned sales agent.

At that period of time, the telecommunications company was going through a transition period and was in a messy state of affairs just like most of the sales guys who worked there.

The alcohol fueled personal lives of the sales team was often overlooked as long as we hit the numbers and we usually did.

The work environment was a pressure cooker and it smelled of cigarettes, cheap cologne and stale beer and one afternoon I left for lunch and never returned.

During the last two years I lived at the house apartment, I made do without heat or electricity and ate mostly canned food. It was now my milestone birthday.

This birthday seemed different. From the night before, I was still intoxicated. I looked around the apartment and realized just how pathetic it all was. I had one loveseat and a few blankets and a battery powered lamp and two jugs of vodka.

All at once, I felt the soulless emptiness within myself. All the years of crap emptied into the septic tank of my head. I was sick of all of it and sick of myself and decided that I had to stop drinking.

A few days later, I moved out of the apartment to disentangle myself from the guttersnipe property owner. He was attracted to me and I wanted no part of him or to the place that had become my tomb.

Chapter 24: Plastic Trees

By now, I had been sober for a while and discovered a house to rent. In an effort to save the world, I had started working in the field of human services as a case manager in a large city. Case managers are assigned a “case load” of dozens of people. Being a case manager means that you meet with people, usually on a monthly basis, to make sure they are doing what they are supposed to be doing and keeping an eye on them professionally speaking.

I sometimes thought that someone should be keeping an eye on some of the case managers themselves. Some of their lives mirrored the chaos of the clients. I heard the stories of some case managers still living the party lifestyle of drinking and clubbing during the week.

These same case managers would complain about the clients doing the exact same thing when they spotted one another at the clubs.

In yet another effort to save the world, I worked as an alcohol counselor in a prison. I like to think that I helped some of the inmates and I learned a lot too. When lunching with some of my fellow alcohol counselors, I heard stories about some of them going out to dinner and drinking too much and then driving home in a frenzied state of mind.

As an alcohol counselor in a prison, getting drunk driving would be very bad indeed. As ridiculous as it sounds, I was the only alcohol counselor who didn't drink and I never published that for fear of being shunned.

I believe some people enter the human services profession to mask their own issues. I believe most of this takes place on a subconscious level and people probably don't realize why they chose that particular career path in the first place.

Working in the human services profession, I discovered that I had more in common with people than I thought I would. Of course, some of the things the inmates did were reprehensible.

The inmates I worked with had alcohol and drug abuse as a contributing factor in their incarceration.

Of course, that doesn't absolve the behavior and the individual must take responsibility.

I thought back to all the times I drove drunk. I was fortunate that I never hurt anybody. I could have easily ended up in prison if something bad had happened. As far as the clients in the large city, I pulled some shady shit too, often to feed my addiction.

After giving up trying to change the world, I entered the sales arena with a sober mind. In the study of human interactions, the dynamic between the role of salesman and the role of case manager and the role of alcohol counselor is not that much different.

In all these roles, I was essentially trying to convince people to do something they did not want to do. One sales company I worked for was a cult on a superficial level. One of the trainers emphasized the point by saying this was a different type of cult…ture and he was serious.

The company was all about groupthink and conformity. It was an altered sense of reality with some people claiming they were still in an extended "honeymoon phase" even after working there for years. Rubbish and hogwash. In the midst of the great migration of working from home, few people willingly offered to return to the office when asked.

As ridiculous as it sounds, I was derided by some of the folks there because I didn't drink. Drinking was a big part of the company culture with alcohol fueled company functions and drinking events commonplace. When it was all said and done, I was happy to get away from that pretend world.

Next, I entered the exciting world of COBRA. Most people think of COBRA as that really expensive insurance that is offered to people between jobs.

Like most jobs in the insurance industry, there's a lot to it and sometimes we had to play the role of phone counselors. Even with our vast knowledge of the COBRA program and all the resources at our disposal, trying to help consumers navigate the health insurance stratosphere was challenging.

I felt especially bad for elderly consumers with the burden of insurance thrust upon them.

So like a child whose head spins around after being possessed, I wanted to save the world again. I vowed to fight for the elderly and shifted my life's mission to Medicare sales. Even for people well versed in it, Medicare is difficult to understand. On top of that, Medicare adds a deadline that forces recipients to make a decision. Talk about making things difficult for the Medicare population.

With these different sales roles, I discovered that it's important to stay true to who you are as an individual. Of course, we have to do what our boss says most of the time or we would be out of a job. More importantly, I have learned how to be more empathetic and just cut people more slack.

Chapter 25: The Bully

Behind smoking and obesity, alcohol is the number three killer in terms of preventable deaths. Like many alcohol abusers, I smoked a lot and my diet was poor including a diet of canned food for years.

For alcohol abusers, the risk oftentimes is three fold as we drink too much, smoke too much, and maintain a poor diet. Alcohol is such a large part of our society and our families and in some states, like my state of Wisconsin, alcohol is a huge part of the culture.

There is no real talk in the news about the deadly consequences of alcohol abuse. I don’t think many people see alcohol as a drug and it's available just about everywhere. Recovering alcohol abusers like myself are surrounded by it no matter where we go. For a recovering alcohol abuser, something as simple as getting groceries can be a source of stress. Back in my drinking days, I drank while shopping. I would drink several of the small plastic bottles of wine that come in a four pack.

To this day, I still have thoughts about drinking to escape. I call these thoughts the “Bully.”

- **Bully**: “Come on man, just a little taste of wine, what’s the big deal?”
- **Me**: “No way. I almost died from that.”
- **Bully**: “You got it this time, go ahead buddy.”
- **Me**: “Not happening. I got this.”

The “Bully” in the example is my own thoughts. It’s called self-talk. We talk to ourselves all the time and have tons of thoughts every day.

Our self-talk tends to lean negative initially. So, it's important to challenge these negative thoughts.

Like most of us, emotional pain can be overwhelming sometimes. For me, the thought of relief through the bottle enters my mind here and there.

If I started drinking again, it would kill me and it wouldn’t take long. My world of alcohol abuse takes me to some horribly dark places. I call it my dark dark. The realization that alcohol would kill me is still not enough to keep me from drinking again.

There is a book that can help. The book talks about Cognitive Behavioral Therapy (CBT). The book is called “Mind Over Mood: Change How You Feel by Changing the Way You Think” by Dennis Greenberger and Christine Padesky.

Chapter 26: In the Light

My cereal packet family is forever awash in the tragedy of what might have been. There were many things that conspired against it.

Like a disaster, there were a series of events that ultimately led to the downfall. It all started when my parents got married young. Of course, many people get married young and make it work but not here.

After my parents were married, they both lived separate lives with my dad working and participating in after work activities and mother hanging out with her friends after hours when she would waitress.

From the start, the family foundation wasn’t even poured, let alone set. When we moved to the little southern town, the lack of a family foundation was one of the fatal flaws. After we moved, we were far away from extended family, including grandparents, aunts and uncles, cousins, family friends and so on.

Nobody knew anybody in this little town and we really didn't know each other either.

Whatever family cohesion that existed quickly disintegrated into dust as everyone started living separate lives. In the years we lived at the same house, the separation just got worse.

After the family house was sold, my dad got remarried and moved to another town and that was the end of our family as a unit.

The shame of it all is the family has some incredibly strong players but we were never part of the same team. It's hard to think about what might have been without feeling a horrible empty sadness.

Picture yourself on a large ship sailing across the ocean. Do we really have any control if the ship will make it safely to the destination? Our own family ship is similar. On top of that, the family ship may not have anybody navigating it.

Either way, the ship sails on, oftentimes with little direction or no direction at all. If we choose to stay on the family ship, then its destination, or lack thereof, becomes our own.

For a family ship with a capable captain and a competent crew, this may be a wonderful place to relax and read a book and figure out your direction in life. If not, you may want to consider alternative transportation options.

Let's assume that I'm a magic fairy who has mystical powers. These magic powers allow me to go back in time and rejoin my family from the moment I was born. Being a magic fairy, I have the power to change all the things that I have control over.

Even as a magic fairy working my sorcery, however, the family would still be in the same situation as it is today. I was pulled down with the ship. Looking back, I wish I had got off the ship a long time ago. To this day, I still see family passengers, just not on that blasted ship.

Back in the day, I tried to avoid dealing with my emotional quagmire. In the madness, I dug myself a deep hole by making poor life decisions and by using destructive addictive forces.

Now, I've been steadily excavating my ancient ruins and still have a long way to go. If I hadn't made a change, I would have been gone a long time ago, and even when I was alive, I was mostly dead on the inside.

After twelve years of riding the wagon, I like to think that my life is slowly moving in a positive direction.

Thank you for joining me on this journey. Delving into the past can be a difficult experience but it need not be a tragedy. Each situation, such as mine, such as yours, is unique. The only real tragedy is not learning to overcome our own discarded darkness.

Goodbye for now.

Recommend Readings

1. Born To Win by Muriel James and Dorothy Jongeward
2. Discarded Darkness: Life Lessons of a Broken Child by Mike Hupfer
3. Feeling Good: The New Mood Therapy by David D. Burns
4. Games People Play: The Psychology of Human Relationships by Eric Berne
5. Getting Sober: A Practical Guide to Making it through the first 30 Days by Kelly Madigan Erlandson
6. Homecoming: Reclaiming and Healing Your Inner Child by John Bradshaw
7. I'm Ok - You're O" by Thomas A. Harris
8. Mind Over Mood: Change How You Feel by Changing the Way You Think by Dennis Greenberger
9. The Hero Within: Six Archetypes We Live By written by Carol Pearson

Printed in Great Britain
by Amazon

38331243R00078